I WILL BE GOOD

Peig McManus was born in 1939 and grew up in one of the last of Dublin's tenements, under the shadow of the Second World War. She learned early about social barriers and, from a young age, set about a path of community activism and educational reform.

Peig trained as a therapist and worked for many national organisations. She worked in radio and television for many years and pursued studies and practice in homeopathy and meditation.

Now in her eighties, the mother of five recounts her journey to becoming herself in her unforgettable memoir *I Will Be Good*.

I Will Be Good

The Memoir of a Woman Before Her Time

PEIG McMANUS

HACHETTE
BOOKS
IRELAND

First published in 2023 by Hachette Books Ireland
First published in paperback in 2024

A CIP catalogue record for this title is available from the British Library.

ISBN 978 1 39971 586 7

Typeset in Cambria by Bookends Publishing Services, Dublin
Printed and bound in Great Britain by Clays Ltd, Elcograf S.p.A.

Hachette Books Ireland policy is to use papers that are
natural, renewable and recyclable products and made from
wood grown in sustainable forests. The logging and
manufacturing processes are expected to conform to
the environmental regulations of the country of origin.

Hachette Books Ireland
8 Castlecourt Centre
Castleknock
Dublin 15, Ireland

A division of Hachette UK Ltd
Carmelite House, 50 Victoria Embankment, EC4Y 0DZ

www.hachettebooksireland.ie

To the memory of my parents,
Bridget Malone and Christopher Dowdall

Contents

Contents

1

Even So

I heard the sound of marching feet while I was in my mother's womb. Sometimes I find this hard to credit. Europe was on the brink of war. The whole world was on the march.

Even so, I can see the joy in my mother Bridie's face in the sepia photo, taken on a work outing on a fine spring day in 1939. Her head is resting on my dad's shoulder, his arm around her. He's respectable in his dark suit, white shirt, collar and tie, while she is petite and glamorous, her hand resting on her swollen belly. They look like a handsome, carefree couple, although Mam already had primary tuberculosis.

One month later, I was born. Mam said it was cold the day she brought me home to our tenement room on North King Street in Dublin 7. Gran, my dad's mother, had the fire lighting. Mam sat in front of it, cradling me on her lap, heating her hands to warm my cold feet. Very soon I got the hang of things and stretched out my tiny feet to meet her warmed hands. This is an image I have carried with me all my life.

War was declared five months later, on Sunday, 3 September. I was asleep in my pram in Gran's kitchen. The neighbours were gathered around the radio in Gran's shop, listening to Britain's prime minister, Neville Chamberlain, declare war on Germany. Until that minute, they had been hoping for a miracle, praying that somebody would intervene. Gran said that our prime minister, Eamon de Valera – Dev – would keep Ireland out of it. She was right, as usual.

As the war progressed, I played on the floor in the space between the fireplace and the door, watching the smoke billowing from the big chimney of Chivers' jam factory, which loomed in the lane behind our house. I saw the sun making splashes on the floor and the dark coming on. I heard my dad's footsteps creaking on the stairs when he came home from work. I also heard my new sister, May, being born in the summer of 1940. I heard the early-morning risings, slop buckets emptying, children returning from school in the afternoon. Babies crying, babies dying, hunger's cry, love's murmurs. Mam singing 'Stormy Weather'.

The following year, work had become scarce, and thousands of Irish men and women went to England to find work or to join the British forces. My dad wanted to go. Mam said he was like a caged animal cooped up in that tenement room with two small children and another on the way. In later years Mam used to warn us, 'When poverty comes in through the window, love flies out through the door.'

The prospect of war seemed glamorous and heroic. Many young men went, leaving their wives and children behind. The women were not so foolhardy. They didn't want dead heroes.

My sister May and I lay at the bottom of the bed, listening to the whispers, pleadings and angry voices. 'Please, Christy, don't go,' Mam kept saying. Funny how things stick in your mind, even after eighty years.

Dad went. Gran gave him the money. He got a job in a brush factory in London and found lodgings in a working-men's hostel called Rowton House.

For a long time, we heard muffled sobs. Mam didn't want to get out of bed or bake. She stopped singing. It was dark in the room: she wouldn't let Gran open the curtains. Gran and Aunt Dolly, my dad's sister, minded us. Gradually they persuaded Mam to get out of bed and open the curtains. Light crept slowly back into our lives. Perhaps she was sad because when she was born in November 1916 her father was in France fighting in the First World War. Now, in November 1941, she was expecting her third baby and her husband was gone. She was worried he might never come back.

Mam was delicate. She had tuberculosis. When she brought my baby brother, Billy, home from hospital, I heard people whispering, 'She won't live to rear him.' Billy was the light of her life. She had wanted a boy. I watched her as she sang 'You Are My Sunshine', filling the room with smoke from her Woodbine cigarettes, daring God to come and get her.

I followed her around. Up the stairs to the landing to fetch water. Down the stairs to empty the slop bucket. I stood on a chair at the table, helping her to make the brown bread. She washed me and May, up as far as possible and down as far as possible. I sat beside her on the bed while she fed the baby. I knew her every mood.

Sometimes Mam let me go down the stairs to Gran and Aunt Dolly's huckster's shop. They sold everything on tick and kept a record of what the customers owed, written on the back of cigarette cartons. Some owed them a lot of money. Gran was always complaining that she would end up in Stubbs. I thought it sounded like a terrible place and was afraid Gran might be sent there. Little did I know that Stubbs was a list of debtors.

I was the apple of Gran's eye. She loved to show me off, standing me on the counter to do a turn for the customers. Smiling through gritted teeth, they would remark, 'Isn't she marvellous? Just like Baby LeRoy', a child actor who was all the rage in American films. And they would add, 'Would ye ever give us ten Woodbines, Dolly, a box of matches and a half-stone of turf? I'll pay ye on Friday.' They had left their children at home and were worried in case they had murdered one another or burned themselves at the open fire.

When we got Dad's wire with his pay on Thursdays, we were in clover. Mam would be in a good humour. She put money by for the rent, the gas, turf for the fire and food, though she still always had to get cigarettes on tick from Gran. Even so, we always had a treat on Thursday.

We were now living in what was called the Emergency. Food, clothing, gas and fuel were rationed. Malnutrition, tuberculosis and many other illnesses were raging through the tenements. In this darkness, kindness weaved her magic spell. Having little, we all shared what we had. Mrs Dempsey, who lived on the top floor, was blind. Somebody gave her a dinner every day and emptied her slop bucket. We learned to mind each other.

We had food supplements, which were distributed through the dispensaries, delights such as cod liver oil, an iron tonic known as Parrish's Food and the dreaded Senokot. We hated cod liver oil, but the Parrish's Food helped to take the bad taste away. DDT, a pesticide, was also supplied. This was a white powder meant to kill the hoppers and fleas, which were spreading disease. I can still remember the smell.

Every Saturday morning, Dubliners had their own form of colonic irrigation. The Senokot tablets were administered, whether they were needed or not, and most of the tenements had only one outdoor toilet. On Saturday mornings, our newly found tolerance was sorely tested.

People sang:

Run, rabbit,
Run, rabbit,
Run, run, run ...

Although Ireland was neutral in the war, there still was a risk of stray German bombs. An air-raid shelter was built on the road outside our house, where ladders, buckets and a pump were stored – the equipment that would be needed if a bomb should fall. The blackouts protected us: curtains were drawn, not a chink of light to be seen. One careless act could endanger the lives of everybody. Despite all the precautions, bombs were accidentally dropped on Dublin's North Strand, just a stone's throw from our house. We lived in fear of it happening again.

Gas rationing was enforced. We could use gas for two hours in the morning and evening but afterwards, with a 'glimmer' of gas left in the pipes, you could take a chance on making a cup of tea. Woe betide you if the Glimmer Man, who always seemed to be lurking in doorways, caught you. Then you weren't allowed to cook for days.

One Thursday, Mam, in a fit of extravagance, bought herself a lamb chop and tried to cook it on the glimmer. I was put out on the landing to keep watch. Then the cry went up on the street. 'Glimmer Man!' I shouted.

Mam switched off the gas. She cooled the ring in the basin, dried it and put it back on the cooker. She was lighting a fag to cover the smell when he knocked. 'Come in,' she called. He entered sniffing and went to feel the ring. He looked around the room, at Billy lying on the bed, at us two small children hanging onto Mam's skirt. He looked into Mam's grey eyes and left. Mam cooked the chop and gave little pieces to May and me, but we were afraid to eat it in case the Glimmer Man came back.

The neighbours gathered in the shop to listen to Gran's radio. All the major cities in Britain were being bombed. Thousands of men, women and children had to sleep in air-raid shelters, like the one outside our door, for weeks on end. They kept up their spirits by singing:

> *Pack up your troubles in your old kit-bag*
> *And smile, smile, smile.*

Or

> *Roll out the barrel, we'll have a barrel of fun.*

The same songs we sang at weddings, wakes and funerals.

The war cast its long shadow over our house. We heard of the thousands of men killed in action, of the missing and the wounded. Mrs Cadbury, who lived above us, received a telegram informing her that her husband had been killed in an air raid in London. The neighbours mourned with her, and worried about their own husbands. Mam told me my dad was in a place where bombs didn't fall, and God would keep him safe.

I enjoyed escaping downstairs, being spoiled by Aunt Dolly and Gran in the shop. Mam wasn't well. Everybody said she would die. I continued to sing and dance for the customers and listen to Gran's running commentaries on them – earwigging, she called it: 'Here's that bloody aul wan looking for snuff on tick. She never paid her bill last week.'

Gran said I'd been on the earth before – I could even hear the grass growing, she added. Strange, because I was hard of hearing even then. I wondered why God didn't make Mam better and bring Dad home.

2

In the Clover

The telegram boy caught us off guard that Saturday morning when he pushed the door open and parked his bike beside the baby's pram in the long, narrow hall. His footsteps clattered on the bare boards, breaking the silence of the sleeping house. His dark uniform cast a shadow on the landing window as he climbed the two flights of stairs to our room. The loud knock startled us, making the baby wail.

'Who in the name of God can that be?' Mam asked.

A louder rap-rap-rap.

'Hold on, hold on. I'll be with you in a minute. Who is it?'

'The telegram boy.'

'You're in the wrong place, son. We got our wire on Thursday.'

'Is this Dowdalls'?' he shouted.

'Yes, but we got ours on Thursday.'

'This is another one.'

'No, it couldn't be. I told you, we got ours on Thursday.'

'Could ye please open the door? I'm in a hurry.'

Mam threw a cardigan over her nightdress and opened the door, still in her bare feet. He shoved the telegram into her hand.

'Are ye sure?' she asked.

'Look at the name. Dowdall. You have to sign for it. Here's a pencil.'

Mam's hands were shaking as she took the telegram and held the paper against the wall to sign for it. Taking his pencil, the telegram boy, his hat perched on the side of his head, his silver buttons shining in the semi-darkness, turned and clattered back down the stairs, whistling.

Closing the door, Mam stood holding the telegram, whispering, 'Jesus, Jesus.' Then she propped it against the brass clock that sat in the centre of the mantelpiece, between the oil lamp and a framed photo of Mam and Dad, which had been taken when they were young. Billy was crying. Mam pulled back the curtain, wakening May, who was conked out beside Billy in the big double bed where we all slept. There was more room now that Dad was gone. Still, I missed him. Mam no longer sang, 'I'll be glad when you're dead, you rascal, you!'

'Hold the baby while I dress meself and make his bottle,' she said to me. 'Your granny will be up.'

Soon I was feeding Billy while Mam went down to the yard to empty the slop bucket and fill the water jug for the breakfast. She made porridge and tea. May and I sat on the side of the bed and ate our breakfast from the wooden table. Mam sat in Dad's chair. When we'd finished, I changed the baby's nappy while Mam cleared off the table, washed the dishes in the basin, dried them and put them away. She swept the floor and cleaned out the grate. Then she emptied the basin into the bucket and filled it with fresh water to wash May and the baby and told me to give myself a lick. As Mam was combing the tangles out of my hair, we heard a door slam and the stairs creak.

'Here's your granny. Stay quiet.'

We listened as the slow steps came nearer. Mam's mouth was set in a straight line. Gran arrived, her small, round body tightly bound in a wraparound apron, her black hat jammed on her head.

'What's wrong, Bridie?' she asked, pushing her way into the room. 'I'm always the last to hear. A customer told me you got a telegram.'

'There it is on the mantelpiece. I haven't opened it yet.'

'I'll open it,' she said, moving towards the fireplace.

'No, you won't,' Mam said, blocking her way. 'I'll open it when I'm good and ready.'

'He's *my* son.'

'And he's my husband, and you're the one who gave him the money to go.' Mam's grey eyes were like shiny stones. I thought she was going to slap Gran.

'Bridie,' Gran said, moving towards her.

'Just go,' Mam shouted.

11

'At least let me take the baby.'

'Just leave us alone. Haven't you taken enough already?'

Gran stood there for a long time staring at Mam before she turned and gave me and May a hug. She kissed the baby and left. I think she was crying.

Mam lit a cigarette and took the telegram over to the window, holding it up to the light, turning it over and over.

'Please, Mam, open it. Is Dad all right? Mrs Hibbits got a telegram when Mr Hibbits was killed, and the Brannigans got one when their Billy was killed. You told me Dad was in a place where the bombs didn't fall. Are you going to open it, Mam?'

She didn't hear me, so I pulled at her skirt.

'Don't be bothering me, child. I can't hear meself thinking.' She slapped me and pushed me away. I started to cry. She scooped me up into her arms, sat me on her lap, held me and rocked me until I stopped. 'I'm sorry, love. I think we all need a breath of fresh air. Would you like to go to the Temple?'

She put on May's coat. Then she dressed the baby, carried him down the stairs and put him in his pram. I held May's hand in case she fell.

The street was alive with women and children doing their Saturday-morning shopping. With the money wired from England, they could now use their ration books to buy tea and sugar, butter, condensed milk, flour, oil, candles and coal. They released pledges from the pawn – locks, blankets, wedding rings, Sunday clothes.

Mrs Brannigan saw us as we passed Mamie Ennis's vegetable shop. She knew what it was like to get a telegram out of the blue. After her husband was killed, the neighbours emptied her slop bucket, carried her water and minded her children until she could lift her head again.

'Are you all right, Bridie?'

'Grand, grand. I'm in a hurry. I'll see you later.'

We pushed the pram, with May sitting at the end holding on to the handle, on up North King Street and past the air-raid shelter where the 'bogey man' lived. We passed Jack's Milk Bar where Mam had bought us pink cake with white icing the previous Thursday, and the bookie where Dad studied form. Pretending not to see the sympathetic glances, we turned onto Henrietta Place and up the hill into Temple Gardens. Mam sat on the bench, smoking. May and I danced on the red-gold leaves, or 'God's magic carpet', as Gran called it. We played chasing and rolled down the grassy bank.

My dad had told me this was the park where I'd taken my first steps into his arms. I was his favourite, Mam said. On Saturday nights, he would sing me to sleep. I still remember the words:

> *Lulla, lulla, lulla, lulla, bye-bye*
> *Do you want the moon to play with*
> *Or the stars to run away with?*
> *They'll come if you don't cry.*

I worried that I would never see him again.

Mam called us: it was time for the baby's bottle. Darkness was falling as we pushed the pram home. The paper boys were singing in loud chorus, trying to outdo each other:

'Extra! Extra! Read all about it! Thousands killed in England.'

'Extra! Extra! Read all about it! Thousands missing, feared dead.'

'Will you, for God's sake, hurry up?' Mam said, as she pushed the pram faster and faster down North King Street. As we opened the hall door, we heard a melodeon playing and people singing: 'The bells are ringing for me and my gal ...'

'Oh, I forgot Fanny Adams was getting married today,' Mam said. She had given Fanny our clothing coupons towards her wedding suit, and the other neighbours had used their rations for the wedding breakfast. The music filled our room as Mam lit the gas mantles and the oil lamp.

In the dim light, I could see her looking at the telegram. Billy started to cry. She made his bottle and fed him. Then she heated the 'blind' stew – a stew that had no meat. She kept looking at the mantelpiece. Her hands were shaking. The clock chimed.

'Bloody clock,' she said, 'chiming our life away.'

Dad had bought it when he had money. It had to be wound every night and polished on Saturdays.

'That clock is out of place in this room,' Mam used to say.

'It's for our new home. It will bring us good luck.' Dad wouldn't part with it.

Mam moved the telegram to wind the clock.

'Please, Mam, open it,' I said.

She looked at me for a long time. She wound the clock and put it back. She lit a cigarette.

'Please.' I touched her arm.

'All right, then, love. It's now or never.'

She got a knife and slid it under the flap. I watched her face.

'Is Da dead?'

'No, love. He's still alive. Alive and kicking.' She had that faraway look. 'That bloody man – he gave me an awful fright.'

'Is he coming home, Mam?'

'I don't know, love.'

'Is he in the clover, Mam?' I joked, trying to make her smile.

'That man would bet on two flies going up a wall. For once his horse came in.'

'Will he be home for Christmas?'

'Will you stop asking questions? I can't hear myself thinking. He gave me such a fright.'

She sighed and rubbed a hand across her forehead.

Then she lifted May onto her lap and put her arm around me. 'I want you to be good girls and mind the baby for me. I have to tell your gran and Aunt Dolly the good news. Don't go near the lamp, do you hear me?'

'Will you bring us back something nice?'

'Only if you're good girls.'

May was sitting on the floor, playing with her rag doll. I was sitting on the bed beside the baby, listening to the dancing feet tapping on the ceiling. They were singing one of Dad's songs, 'Underneath the Arches', about dreams being dreamed away.

'I won't be long,' Mam said, as she closed the door.

3

I Will Be Good

At the end of her tether, Mam would shout up the chimney, 'Santa, don't bring Peggy Dowdall any toys. She's too bold,' and mutter to herself, 'Dear God, what am I going to do with that child?'

I would shout up, 'Please, Santa, I will be good, I will be good. Just bring me a mama doll.'

My sister would shout up, 'Please bring me a mama doll. I am good.'

In my child's mind, Santa, Baby Jesus and Holy God came down from the heavens, strung together with tinsel, lit by candlelight, Santa guiding them through the snow on his reindeer to the tunes of 'Jingle Bells', 'Away in a Manger' and 'Silent Night'. Santa bringing feelings of joyous anticipation. Baby Jesus bringing sadness because he had nowhere to lay his sweet head, except in a freezing barn with only cows to keep him warm. Holy God keeping score of whether we were good, very good, bold or very bold.

So, the first Christmas I remember was during the Second World War, wondering if Santa would make it from the North Pole through the bombing. Europe lay in tatters. Many little children had no place to lay their heads. The adults said we were lucky to be alive. They worried about food and fuel rations, and telegrams from England. Still they sang 'White Christmas'.

On Christmas Eve, the women in our house washed, scrubbed and polished windows, landings, stairs, hallways and rooms until the bare boards were milk white and the windows gleamed. Clocks, newly released from the pawn, sat ticking, reminding us of when our dads would be coming home from England. Most of the men who lived in our house were expected home. They came from the boats, carrying their cardboard cases, tired and hungry.

I had never seen my mam kiss my dad like that before. They sat at the table, smiling at each other. May and I climbed onto Dad's lap and asked him if he had seen Santa. Would he be able to make it down our chimney in the blackout? Dad said not to worry: he'd heard that Santa was on his way. He would have no bother getting down our chimney, but we had to leave a bottle of stout and some Christmas pudding out for him.

Dad went downstairs to see Gran and Aunt Dolly. It was growing dark. Mam lit the oil lamp and bathed me, May and Billy in the tin bath in front of the fire. When Dad came back he said Gran would mind us while he and Mam went to the pub – all our aunts, uncles and neighbours gathered in Vaughan's pub for a sing-song on Christmas Eve.

Gran put us to bed, but we couldn't sleep. We were listening for the sound of Santa's sleigh on the roof. Above us, we could hear children's voices echoing through the house, shouting, fighting, laughing, crying, all waiting for Santa.

Our room was dark, cosy and smoky. Gran sat drinking a bottle of stout beside the fire. She told us Mam had sent a letter to Santa. He knew May and I wanted mama dolls and Billy was getting a toy drum. The quicker we went to sleep, she said, the quicker Santa would come. We said our prayer:

> Oh, Angel of God, my guardian dear,
> To whom God's love commits me here.
> Ever this day, be at my side,
> To light and guard, to rule and guide. Amen.

Gran's shadow grew dimmer and we drifted off to the Land of Nod.

May woke first. 'Oh, Peggy, look what Santa brought us.' There, snuggled between us, lay two dolls in shiny white dresses. We cuddled and kissed them, and squashed them until they squeaked 'Mama.' Billy woke and found the drum.

The noise of the drum and the dolls awakened Mam and Dad, who were sleeping at the top of the bed. 'Go back to sleep. It's the middle of the night,' they said. We played as quietly as we could until the whole house echoed with the noise of whistles and drums, skipping ropes, marbles, swords, guns, trains, rocking-horses and shouts of 'Look what Santa brought me!'

Soon we heard the footsteps of families on their way to early-morning Mass in St Michan's, which was on Halston Street just across the road. We wrapped our dolls up nice and warm, and showed them to the Baby Jesus in the crib at the church. I called my doll Rosebud and May called hers Molly.

In the afternoon, we went down to Gran, who was making the Christmas dinner. Her room was filled with steam and smoke. The goose was hanging upside down, roasting over the open fire.

The three of us were put sitting on Gran's big brass bed in the middle of pillows, bolsters and grey army coats. A paradise of hills, valleys, nooks and crannies, which muffled the sound of Billy's drum and the squeaky Mama cries.

After dinner, the table was shoved against the bed to make room for the hooley. Dad and Uncle Paddy, my dad's brother, who was home on leave from the Irish Army, were dancing and singing 'Underneath the Arches' when I discovered a lump on Rosebud's back.

Aunt Dolly was singing 'Love's Last Word Is Spoken (Chérie)' when I swiped a knife from the table and ripped the back of Rosebud's dress. I pulled out a shiny box, leaving a gaping hole in Rosebud's back. She had lost the power of speech.

I howled.

'What's wrong, child?' Gran asked. 'God almighty, would ye look what that young wan is after doing?' There I sat, Rosebud's voice box in my hand, trying to hide the hole in her back.

'How did ye manage that?' Mam asked.

'Why did you do it?' Dad asked.

'I don't know,' I sobbed.

'She's a most destructive child,' Gran said. 'What's to be done with her?'

Aunt Dolly, my godmother, came to the rescue. 'Leave her alone. She's just a child. I remember,' she said, pointing at Uncle Paddy, '*he* tore the hair out of my doll.' She was just getting started on one of her 'I remember's, which always lasted a long time and got on everybody's nerves.

'That's enough,' Gran said. 'It's Christmas Day, for God's sake.'

Aunt Dolly picked me up and cradled me against her soft body. I sat on her lap, clutching Rosebud and her voice box. I knew what I had done came under the heading of 'very bold'.

The hooley resumed.

Gran sang 'The Tri-Coloured Ribbon'.

Mam sang 'The Little Shirt My Mother Made for Me'.

They seemed to have forgotten what I had done. Aunt Dolly said she would put me to bed. Mam said she would be up later with May and Billy. Aunt Dolly lit the lamp. 'You're not a bad girl,' she said softly.

'I'm sorry,' I said. 'I will be good.'

'I know, love. Just say your prayers.'

I asked Holy God to make Rosebud better.

Next morning, I wakened early. The light filtered through a gap in the curtain, revealing Rosebud lying beside me in her shiny white dress. Someone had put her back together. Cautiously, I turned her over. She squeaked, 'Mama.' Quickly I pushed her under the covers. I wondered who had fixed her – Holy God? Baby Jesus? Aunt Dolly? Or even Gran?

From a distance it doesn't matter. I knew I had been forgiven. A good job: I never learned how to be a good girl. Eventually I stopped trying and just became myself.

4

Dandelions through the Letterbox

Mam was distraught when the doctor told her I had pneumonia. He could do no more for me. I was in God's hands now. For the next forty-eight hours, I hovered between life and death. Mam fed me on sips of brandy and water. She told me I kept saying, 'Don't give me that stuff in the bottle.' I meant the brandy. In later years, I grew quite fond of it.

I was in a cold, dark place. I wanted to leave but I knew Mam couldn't bear it. Gran, Aunt Dolly and all the neighbours were praying for me. Slowly I came back to life. Gran said it was a miracle. Now they had to build up my strength. Every day I had to swallow a raw egg with warm milk and sugar. I can still feel the slimy taste in my mouth. To this day, the sight of a runny egg turns my stomach.

May, Billy and I were still sucking dummies. We were always dropping them on the floor and putting them back into our mouths, filthy dirty. Mam said they were causing disease and would have to go. Dad took matters in hand. One Sunday morning he brought the three of us down the stairs, out to the toilet in the backyard. He took the dummies out of our mouths, threw them into the toilet and pulled the chain. We howled as we watched them disappearing down the brown-stained pot. 'Now,' he said, pointing, 'if you want your dummies, you'll have to go down there for them.'

Mam said we howled for three days and nights. I imagine it must have been like addicts going cold turkey.

Despite the removal of the dummies, we developed impetigo. Big, pus-filled scabs spread over our bodies. They were highly contagious and had to be scrubbed every night with carbolic soap. We all had to have our heads shaved, including Mam, her shiny black hair gone. She wore a hat to hide her bald head. Aunt Dolly made cloth coverings for our hands to stop us from scratching and spreading the disease. Even as a small child, I knew there was something shameful about the ugly scabs.

Our sores eventually healed. Our hands were freed, our hair grew. Mam sang 'Bye Bye Blackbird' and our cares and woes were packed away for a while.

I was four years old when I developed a cough. An X-ray revealed that I had a shadow on my lung. It was decided the best course of action was to remove my tonsils.

Tonsillectomies were fashionable at the time. May and Billy had their perfectly healthy tonsils removed as a precaution. I was sent to Cheeverstown Convalescent Home to recuperate.

When I came home, I had a new brother. He was called Christopher after my dad. I begged Mam to let me hold him. She put me sitting on the bed. She warned me that if he felt too heavy, I was to fall backwards onto the bed and not to drop him on the floor. He was dressed in a lacy shawl and hat that Aunt Dolly had made for him. There were tufts of black hair sticking out through his cap. He wasn't as wriggly as the cat. I heard Mam telling Aunt Dolly that she thought Christopher had gastroenteritis. A spurt of green diarrhoea shot out of his bottom when the nurse was weighing him. Mam was right. Christopher died a fortnight later. Dad carried him in a white coffin on his bike up to Glasnevin, where he was buried in the Angels' Plot.

Mam blamed the rats for spreading disease. She was afraid to go to sleep because she could hear them at night, scurrying around. Nothing was safe. Babies' bottles, food – they even dragged dirty nappies down the rat holes. She couldn't wait to get out of North King Street. She said we were in limbo land, waiting for the key to our new house. Meantime she had another baby, called Anne. There was something wrong with her heart. Anne lived for six months. She died in hospital the week we got the key to our new home.

We had been promised a new house with a flush toilet and a bath, our own sink and a garden in which we could grow food. We were just waiting for the key. Our name, Dowdall, was at the top of the corporation housing list because my mam had tuberculosis, which was the plague of Ireland at that time. The tenements were dark, rat-infested and overcrowded, with large families living in one room. Most of the buildings had only one toilet in the yard which was shared between at least twenty people. They were breeding grounds for gastroenteritis, impetigo, scabies, tuberculosis, scarlet fever and, of course, there was malnutrition. Desperate mothers foraged daily for food to feed all those hungry little sparrows. Unemployment was rife, which was why so many men had to go to England to find work.

Now, though, our dad was home, and we were all waiting to move to Cabra to make a new life.

The sounds of love and birth, sorrow and death, echoed through the house. I can still hear the songs they sang: 'We'll Gather Lilacs in the Spring' and 'We'll Meet Again'.

My dad sang, 'Lulla, lulla, bye-bye' to me.

Such hopes and dreams. We shared our joys, our sorrows and our food: a cup of sugar, a drop of milk or a few potatoes.

Still, we were moving on, waiting for the key to our new home in Cabra.

Gran said, 'At least it's on the North Side. You'll be able to come and see us.'

I was still spending a lot of time with Gran and Aunt Dolly in their newsagent and tobacco shop, which was just below our room. Mam used to say that they spoiled me rotten. Aunt Dolly backed horses and drank whiskey. She let me help her pick the winners. Sometimes she would swear when her horse didn't win. 'That bastard Richards let me down yesterday.' Even though I was young, I knew Gordon Richards was the jockey and I wondered why Aunt Dolly wasn't cursing the horse. When I tried to explain to my mam that the bastard Richards had let Aunt Dolly down, she slapped me and told me not to be using such bad language. I told her to buck off. Mam was raging. That night, as I lay at the bottom of the bed, I heard her saying to Dad, 'The sooner we get out of here the better. Your sister and mother are a very bad influence on my child. I can't believe the language that comes out of her mouth.'

Someone in the corporation must have heard Mam because we got the key the next week.

At that time Cabra West, a brand new housing estate, was out in the country. Gran and Aunt Dolly waved us goodbye on a fine spring day as we set off on our journey to inspect our new house. It seemed a very long walk to the bus stop, but May and I, then aged three and four, were full of excitement and skipped along ahead of our parents. Billy, aged two, was delicate and cried for Mam. Dad had to lift him onto the number 22 bus in Dorset Street and carry him up the stairs. Billy sat on Mam's lap, afraid to move.

May and I ran to the front seat of the bus and saw the half-demolished houses on Dorset Street, with no roofs, the stairways pointing up to the sky. The slums were being cleared. We were joining the vast throng of Dubliners leaving their rat-infested tenements and moving to new homes on the city's outskirts. We turned onto the North Circular Road. Dad pointed out the Mater Hospital, Mountjoy Jail, Phibsborough Church and the rows of neat town houses, all built a hundred years before. We were leaving old Dublin behind and entering virgin territory.

We turned into Carnlough Road, the entrance to Cabra West. It was raw, with rows and rows of grey pebble-dashed houses that seemed to go on and on for ever. We travelled through the maze of houses until the bus conductor announced Fassaugh Avenue. Dad said, 'This is where we get off.' He carried Billy down the stairs while Mam descended ahead of us girls to make sure we didn't fall.

Our new house was on Broombridge Road, at the top of the hill. It seemed such a long way from the bus stop. Dad said we could see all over Cabra from it. We had our own hall door, our own brass letterbox, a knocker and a side entrance. Dad turned the key in the lock and we entered our new home. We ran up the wooden stairs, which were just inside the hall door. Mam showed us what she said was the bathroom. There was a toilet and a bath. We'd never seen a bath before! We turned on the taps. We pulled the toilet chain. We listened to the sound of running water, and bathed in the sunlight shining through the frosted-glass window.

We went into the back bedroom, our very own room, where May, Billy and I were to sleep. From our window we could see the long back garden, ablaze with yellow flowers. Dad said they were dandelions.

'Come and look at our bedroom, Bridie,' Dad said, herding us into the front bedroom. It was a big room with a wooden press and a fireplace. From the window we could see rows and rows of half-built houses.

Dad said to Mam, 'It won't look so bad out there when all the building's finished.'

The kitchen and the parlour were downstairs. From the big kitchen window, we could see the back garden and the dandelions. We just wanted to get out there. Mam unlocked the back door and shouted, 'Be careful! Don't fall!' as we trundled down the steps.

We threw ourselves down among the dandelions, pulling off their heads. We scrunched the long green stalks and rubbed the white sap on Billy. They didn't smell nice.

May and I plucked armfuls of dandelions and ran through the side entrance to the front door. We stood on our tippy toes and shoved them in through the letterbox. Mam and Dad, who were sitting on the stairs, could see them dropping into the hall. They laughed and shouted, 'Stop! Stop! You'll have the place destroyed before we move in.'

The dandelions were still blooming when we finally moved to Cabra that summer – we learned they were weeds, also called 'piss-in-the-bed'. They had to be cleared out so that we could grow food.

We learned a lot that summer. Cabra West was called the Wild West, a rough place. It was teeming with hordes of children and poverty-stricken people living from hand to mouth, like the rest of Europe, and striving to learn how to live together to create a brave new world. Dad said we would live there until we got something better. He warned us not to make free with the neighbours, or 'they'll end up living in our ear' and 'looking for a loan of our pig's cheek to graze their cabbage'.

Others were not so disenchanted and sang on the bus on Saturday nights after they'd had a few jars:

> *With someone like you, a pal so good and true,*
> *I'd like to leave it all behind, and go and find*
> *Some place that's known to God alone,*
> *Just a spot to call our own.*
> *We'd find perfect peace,*
> *Where joys never cease,*
> *Out there beneath a kindly sky,*
> *We'd build a sweet little nest, out there in*
> > *Cabra West*
> *And let the rest of the world go by.*

Mam was sick again. Dad furiously attacked the tangled masses of weeds and dandelions, daisies, poppies and buttercups. He tried to cultivate the garden, but he was a city dweller and didn't know where to start. Gran loaned him the money for a fork, a spade and a rake. The weeds lay in tumbles in the garden, while Dad tried to figure out what to do with them.

Meantime, we made free with the neighbourhood kids, swinging on the lamp posts, skipping, playing piggy beds, relievio, doctors and nurses. The boys made war with the other boys who lived on Carnlough Road, then played football with them. The girls held hands in a circle and danced around singing,

Ring a ring o' roses, a pocket full of posies
Atishoo, atishoo, we all fall down!

We all fell in a heap on the grass, screaming with laughter. Little did we realise that 'we all fall down' referred to people dying of the Great Plague of London, about three hundred years before.

One day the doctor came to our house with his black bag. Dad was at home and Mam was in bed. We thought he was bringing a baby because he always brought the babies in his black bag. When he left, we ran upstairs. Mam was lying in the bed, crying. We jumped onto the bed and asked, 'Where's the baby?'

Dad shouted, 'Get off that bed. You'll hurt your mother. There is no baby. Your mam is sick and has to go to hospital.' We all started to cry.

Mam said, 'Don't be upset. I'll be home in just a few weeks. Go downstairs while we get things ready. The ambulance will be coming in a few minutes.'

'Is Mam going to die?' May kept saying. Billy was just crying for his mam.

'Shut up. Our mam is not going to die,' I shouted, trying to reassure myself.

Dad got one of the neighbours to mind us, while he took Mam to the hospital.

She was gone for a long time. Nobody told us where she was or when she was coming back. We were minded by the neighbours and Aunt Biddy. Dad said his sister was a cranky old maid. Biddy had been a lady's maid in England and had delusions of grandeur. Dad said she didn't know how to cook, clean or lift anything heavier than a feather duster. She was very religious and used to recite the rosary out loud, all day. The worst part, as far as my dad was concerned, was the sprinkling of the beds with holy water. He said she'd give us all pneumonia.

The spade, the rake and the fork stood idle against the wall in the back porch, while we played cowboys and indians among the mangled wildflowers in the back garden. Dad spent his time cycling to work in the city and cycling to Crooksling Sanatorium in south County Dublin to see Mam. He brought home two cloth dolls, which Mam had made for May and me, and a cloth dog for Billy.

Aunt Biddy walked to school with us, carrying Billy on her back. She idolised him. This was a great source of annoyance to my dad, who claimed that Aunt Biddy was ruining Billy and making him lazy.

We heard our neighbours saying that our mam might never come home again. They whispered that people were dying like flies in Crooksling.

Summer passed and winter came. We slid on the icy roads. The three of us huddled together under grey army coats in the single iron bed the health clinic had given Mam so that she could sleep by herself and not spread disease. The dandelions came again and went, and still no sign of Mam. Although we kind of got used to her not being there, we still longed to see her. We pleaded with Dad to take us to see her but there was no money for the long bus journey. She was so far away, so isolated, hidden out of sight. There was an awful stigma attached to tuberculosis at that time. People had a terrible fear of catching it. It was shameful, called the dirty disease. Mam had warned us time and again that we were not to tell anybody about her illness.

One day, May, Billy and I were sitting on the garden wall, watching the kids swinging on the lamp post. We saw a woman walking up the road from the bus stop. She stood in front of us. We did not recognise her! She started to cry and lifted Billy off the wall. We did not know her because she looked so lovely. I can still remember her shiny black hair and grey-green eyes. Our Mam was back! She had signed herself out of Crooksling Sanatorium against the advice of the doctors, who told her she had only a short time to live.

I wonder how far she had to walk to the bus stop, carrying her brown cardboard suitcase, to catch the bus into the city. How long did she have to wait for the next bus to bring her home to Cabra?

There was great rejoicing in our house that night. Even Dad had not known she was coming home. We were not supposed to touch our mother, but we climbed all over her, afraid she might leave us again. She said we were all filthy and crawling with lice. She washed us in the tin bath and fine-combed our hair. Poor Aunt Biddy got into terrible trouble.

Mam was back and Dad began to tackle the garden again, but he never managed to get the hang of it.

We roamed the fields around Broombridge, which was at the bottom of our road. We trapped bees in jam jars filled with dandelions. We caught minnows in the Tolka river and learned to swim in the Royal Canal, in our knickers, with some tuition from our neighbour Mr Waldron. He would shout, 'Jump!' We would plunge into the six-foot-deep stretch and dog-paddle to the other side. We didn't want to make a show of ourselves if Mr Waldron had to rescue us. There was such a sense of pride when we made it across that narrow stretch of water and scrambled onto the path under the bridge – where Sir Rowan Hamilton, the nineteenth-century astronomer and mathematician, had scratched on the wall his famous formula for quaternion multiplication. I wonder was he cheering us on.

Broombridge Road was special to me, perhaps because it had its own history, but all the other roads had strange names – Bannow Road, Carnlough Road, Ventry Road, Fassaugh Avenue, Killala Road. Later I learned that most of the corporation planners were from the country and had just named the roads after their home places. The guards, teachers, doctors, nurses and rent collectors were mostly from other parts of the country as well. They lived in the private houses. With the best of intentions, the corporation had managed to create ghettos. We learned to be cute when asked where we lived. We always said Phibsborough or the Navan Road, which was considered a more respectable part of the city.

Mam became sick again and spent a lot of time in bed, but she always tried to have our dinner ready when we came home from school. Wednesday was the best day: chips and eggs. Because of Mam's sickness, she got a voucher from the Health Board every week for seven eggs, a pound of butter and three pints of milk.

Our new home was freezing that winter. There were mornings when Dad had to scrape the ice off the windows. Sometimes, we got logs from the local depot and Dad split them in the back yard. I loved to watch him swing the hatchet in the air, though I was afraid he might miss the log. He said that it had to be a clean, clear cut. Mam said that it was dangerous and she implored us to stay inside when Dad was chopping. Naturally we all managed to hide outside and watch.

Dad would light the fire in the small grate in the corner of the room and sit beside Mam on the bed. May, Billy and I sat on logs beside the fire and listened to Mam and Dad singing songs from the old books Gran had given us from the shop. Dad always sang 'Camptown Races' and Mam loved to sing 'Beautiful Dreamer'.

Before we went to bed, Dad would switch off the lights

and the room became full of shadows. In the glow of the firelight, he taught us how to make shapes on the wall with our fingers and thumbs: rabbits, dogs and pussy cats. Dad would bark and meow and make horsey noises. We all joined in, even Mam. Dad told us it was magic. He said that we had the power to make any shape we liked.

5

You Can, But You May Not

These days, I wonder what kind of negotiations and inducements took place behind the scenes for the nuns to accept such a multitude of smelly, snotty-nosed kids from the inner city. In 1835, the Dominican nuns had established a boarding school in Cabra for young ladies from all over the country. In 1846 they started a school for deaf mute girls, as they would have been described then, and later a small school for the local children in Cabra. To accommodate the influx of urchins from the inner city, a new Dominican convent school was built and cordoned off from the boarding school, so that 'never the twain shall meet'.

I started school in 1944 and May started the following year. That September, Mam walked with us to school on our first day back after the summer. She took us into the huge hall and kissed us goodbye. We were brought to our classrooms by a nun. May and I were separated. I was now in high babies class because I was six and May was in low babies. The infant classes were on the bottom floor.

Until I went to the convent, I thought all children were the same and spoke the same language. Very quickly I learned this was not so. One of the little girls was jigging up and down, holding her hands on her wee.

'Please, Miss, can I go to the lav?' she asked.

The teacher answered, 'You can, but you may not.'

The little girl, knowing nothing about grammar, wet the floor. 'You can, but you may not' stuck in my mind for ever.

Infant school passed in a haze for May and me. Even though Mam was home, she still had to spend a lot of time in bed. I was always getting ear infections. This meant that I had a runny ear and I was hard of hearing. I found it difficult to make out what the teachers were saying. I developed a great imagination and tried to anticipate what was being asked of me. As a result, I got a lot of things wrong. For instance, when I was learning the hymns for my first holy communion, I sang:

> Hail, Queen of Heaven, the ocean star,
> Glide of the glanderer here we nown,

> *Thrown on life's surge, we glaim thy glare*
> *Save us from Herod and from woe.*

The one word I was sure was right was Herod because Herod was the man who killed all the babies when Jesus was born. Baby Jesus escaped because he was hiding in the manger with Mary and Joseph. I learned later that the words were 'save us from *peril* and from woe'.

I also picked up some strange information when I moved into the holy communion class the next year. I learned about venial sins, mortal sins, heaven, hell, purgatory and limbo. Heaven was where you went if you had no sins. It was a wonderful place where angels sat on thrones that were covered with jewels, playing harps and singing hymns. Every time you were good on earth, another jewel was added to your throne in heaven. Purgatory was the place you went if you had a few sins, like being disobedient or giving cheek to your mam. It was a miserable, cold place where you had to repent before you were fit for heaven. This could take a very long time, so it was better if you didn't commit any sins and went straight to heaven. Limbo was for people who weren't baptised and would never see the face of God. Even at an early age, I thought this was mean because it included babies and it wasn't their fault that they weren't baptised.

Hell was an awful place, damnation in the eternal flames with dancing devils, who had pitchforks. That's where Aunt Biddy said my dad was going to end up. She also said May and I would end up there, too, if we didn't say our prayers and behave properly. However, I knew I would have to do something very bad before I went to hell. Like killing Aunt Biddy. I often felt like killing her, but that was only a bad thought. A venial sin. Then there were the bad boys who robbed orchards and mitched from school. Those were mortal sins. They were sent to the reformatories in Letterfrack and Dangan and would probably also end up in the burning flames of hell.

May, my clever sister, was so terrified of school she used to be sick every morning. She couldn't read, couldn't write and couldn't concentrate. I suppose both of us were afraid of everything. We didn't learn much in the first few years. At lunch hour, hundreds of mixed infants were released into the huge grey concrete playground. May and I sat huddled on the seat in the long narrow shed watching them running around and banging into each other, the boys fighting, the girls huddling in groups talking, laughing, crying, the noise washing over us, deafening our aloneness.

When the bell rang, silence descended. We got into our lines and marched straight back to our classes. Then the air was filled with the sound of seagulls, as they swirled, dived and fought over the half-eaten sandwiches left behind. Seagulls in those days were supposed to be unlucky. They sounded like the banshee who keened when a person was going to die. When the gulls were screeching, I thought it meant my mam was going to die. Even to this day, I shiver when I hear them.

Eventually, we got the courage to join the playground gangs. We found a little clique of friends. We made our own way to school, joining the hundreds of children meandering in pairs towards the Cabra convent. Emerging onto Ratoath Road in one vast river, we surged to the entrance. The sound of feet and the hum of children's voices filled the air. Suddenly there was silence as we entered the convent gates, lined up and were led into our classes by our teachers.

By now May and I were resigned to our fate. I was waiting to make my communion. Mam still needed to stay in bed a lot of the time. Aunt Biddy insisted on bringing us to school, although we didn't want her to. The other kids used to jeer at her and call her Biddy Burst the Bucket. She looked very old-fashioned in her long dark coat and black hat. We tried to hide and pretend we weren't with her, and sometimes even joined the gang who were taunting her. Not a great spiritual preparation for my communion!

In the first communion class, I was learning how to examine my conscience in order to confess my sins. I was still trying to understand the difference between mortal and venial sins. A mortal sin meant the eternal flames of hell for ever. A venial sin meant purgatory for God 'knows how long'. At least I wasn't going to limbo because I was baptised. If I was good, I would be sent to heaven to sit on a throne for ever and ever with all the other angels. I definitely didn't want to go to hell, but I wasn't sure I wanted to end up sitting on a throne with the good people for ever. I was afraid I might end up beside Aunt Biddy.

At all costs, I was to avoid the devil with all his works and all his prompts. Or pomps! I had no idea what this meant. But the devil was serious, always tempting us to commit mortal sins.

On my first confession, I stumbled into the dark box in a state of total confusion. I had no idea what to say, so I said what I had learned off by heart: 'Bless me, Father, for I have sinned. This is my first confession. I was disobedient and I gave back cheek.'

Aunt Biddy and the nun said that if you made a bad confession, you could end up in the eternal flames for ever. A bad confession was leaving out a serious sin. I knew tormenting Aunt Biddy was a serious sin, but I didn't know how to explain it, so I left it out. Getting the holy communion, which was the body of Christ, stuck in your teeth was the worst sin of all, but that hadn't happened to me yet.

Gran and Aunt Dolly brought me into town to buy my communion clothes. I got a beautiful white dress and shiny shoes. Aunt Dolly made me a cloth bag to collect my money in. When I was all dressed up in my new clothes, May said, 'Oh, Peggy, you look like a queen.'

On the special day of our first holy communion, we were allowed to enter the chapel, which was in the grounds of the private boarding school. I had always wanted to go in: I used to peep through the hedge and admire the beautiful gardens and the tiny chapel. I would watch the girls walking sedately in pairs in their lovely shiny black shoes, their blue gymslips and gold jumpers.

It was a wonderful, joyful time, sitting between my mam and dad, listening to the music, the hymns, and watching the boys and girls parading up to the altar rails to receive their communion. I was praying that the body of Christ would not get stuck in my teeth. Instead, it stuck to the roof of my mouth. Not quite as bad, I thought. I tried to get it off with my tongue while keeping my mouth closed. I walked back down the aisle, hoping no one would notice. Eventually it dissolved into little bits. It was definitely a venial sin, I decided, maybe even a mortal one. Dad said it wasn't a sin at all because I didn't do it on purpose.

The first communion celebration breakfast was held in the nuns' dining hall. The nuns escorted us to our places at the long tables, which were covered with white linen cloths and lace. There were place-names for each family along with silver candlesticks, china cups and saucers, side plates, big plates and beautiful glasses. There were milk jugs, sugar bowls, silver bowls filled with home-made jam, pats of butter, home-made bread and boiled eggs. Dad was fascinated by the special little spoon for the boiled eggs. None of us had ever seen such splendour. At first, we were overawed.

The deaf girls poured water into the lovely glasses so

that we could wash down the body of Christ before eating our food. Then we gave thanks for the food we were about to eat.

Bless us, O Lord, for these thy gifts
Which of thy bounty
We are about to receive,
Through Christ, Our Lord, Amen.

We had big white napkins tucked under our chins so that we wouldn't dirty our clothes. It was lovely and awful. I was afraid of making a show of myself, having no idea which plate or knife to use. Tea was served. Mam cut the top off my egg and made me a butter and jam sandwich. She said I was a good girl because I hadn't spilled anything on my new clothes.

The nuns were kind, but I was dying to get away to Aunt Dolly and Gran to get fizzy lemonade, chocolate biscuits and the money I was going to collect in the bag Aunt Dolly had made for me. That was a most important part of making my holy communion.

Later, Aunt Dolly, Gran and Uncle Paddy each gave me a half-crown, a good start. I gulped down the fizzy lemonade and ate the biscuits.

By now, I was feeling a bit sick and was trying to work out how to collect the money. It was a lovely sunny day. I found a chair and sat in the doorway of Gran's shop. Dressed up in my finery, I was admired by all the customers. In fact, they had no choice because Gran said, 'Isn't she lovely?' to each person as they tried to squeeze past me to get into the shop. Most of them put a hard-earned thrupenny bit into my bag, which was conveniently open. A venial sin, perhaps.

Gran and Aunt Dolly had bought me a bright blue mohair coat, trimmed with velvet. It would see me through the next few winters. I sat sweltering in it, emptying the bag onto my lap and counting my money. By the end of the day, my holy communion dress was black and I had collected two pounds, three shillings and ninepence.

Life is not fair. Next morning, Mam extracted two pounds, two shillings from my bag. I was raging. Mam said I was selfish. She used the money to buy wool to make cardigans for May and me. They were red, knitted in a box stitch. Mam spent hours and hours working on them, but I hated that cardigan. Mam said I was most ungrateful – and me only after making my first holy communion! I was definitely heading for the eternal flames of hell.

Having made my communion, I graduated to second class, which was upstairs with the big girls. My new teacher was called Miss McCarthy. She was an angel. She instilled in me my love of English, poetry and rhyme. I never saw her slap a child or put one in the dunce's corner. Thomas Gray's 'Elegy Written in a Country Churchyard' comes to mind when I think of her. I still remember every line.

The curfew tolls the knell of parting day,
The lowing herd wind slowly o'er the lea …

Dad had also learned that poem in school and he used to recite it with me. Even at such a young age, I felt what it meant. As adults, how little we know of what children understand in their hearts.

Gray's 'Elegy' reminds me of the deaf girls who worked in the background at the convent, cleaning the toilets, the sinks, scrubbing the floors, cooking and washing. We were afraid of them. They made guttural sounds of frustration when we accidentally walked in muddy shoes on the floor they had just scrubbed. Sometimes they pinched us or pulled our hair out of sheer desperation, trying to make themselves understood. They were not much older than us. We thought they were vicious. It was as if they were not really human. I think of them now as Gray's gems and flowers:

Full many a gem of purest ray serene,
The dark unfathom'd caves of ocean bear:
Full many a flower is born to blush unseen,
And waste its sweetness on the desert air.

Miss McCarthy knew everything. She knew who was hungry, sad or fearful. She knew the bullies and the bullied, and she managed it all discreetly. She watched her fifty-six pupils learn to fend for themselves, only intervening when absolutely necessary. She must have missed the Sheila Fish episode, though. In our class there were the popular girls who were full of themselves. Everyone wanted to belong in that group, or at least not to get on the wrong side of it. Then there were the unwashed and the shunned. I hovered somewhere in the middle, longing to become part of the in-group.

Sheila Fish was one of the shunned. She crept into the class like a mouse. Sometimes she smelt because her ma was dead. Her bald, scabby head was covered with a scarf. Nobody, including me, wanted to sit with her. One day while we were saying our prayers, one of the popular girls pulled off Sheila's scarf. There she stood, her bald, scabby head exposed to the whole class. I knew this was a sin. I was ashamed for Sheila Fish, ashamed for myself. I knew what it was like to have my head shaved. Yet I said nothing. Miss McCarthy must have been preoccupied. It had all happened in a flash, amid stifled giggles.

Sheila must have been a Stoic in her former life. I saw the tears falling on her desk. She just put her scarf back on and quietly continued her prayers.

When prayers ended, Sheila put up her hand and asked Miss McCarthy, '*An bhfuil cead agaim dul amach?*' We were learning Irish and way past the stage of saying, 'Can I go to the lav, Miss?' Though I don't think Miss McCarthy would ever have said to a child, 'You can, but you may not.'

I would love to say that I made friends with Sheila, but I didn't. She moved into another class. Eventually her hair grew back.

Miss McCarthy was way ahead of her time. She instilled in us a wish to say, 'Yes, I can'. She promoted in me a love of learning. Years later, when I was studying shorthand, typing and English at a local technical college, I had another inspiring teacher. She taught me 'Ozymandias', by Percy Bysshe Shelley.

'My name is Ozymandias, king of kings:
Look on my works, ye Mighty, and despair!'

These words were inscribed on the remains of a statue half-sunk in desert sands, reminding us that all kinds of power are only temporary on this earthly journey. We all end up in the same way. Power can be used in many ways. 'You can, but you may not.'

6

Earning My Keep

Even while we were still in primary school, Dad believed that children should earn their keep and face reality as soon as possible. He made us aware of this before we could walk and talk. I used to wonder when it would happen.

Meantime we went out to play. During the long summer holidays, gangs of kids were sent out and told not to come back until they were called for. From early morning until late at night we played skipping, chasing, cowboys and Indians, nick-nack knocking on doors, annoying anybody and everybody. We caught bees in jam jars, collected frog spawn in milk bottles, chased minnows into the rushes with sacks and tried to sell them to other kids.

Wild, untamed and curious, we roamed around Cabra West, searching for adventure and money. Mostly we needed money. We wanted to break loose and get out into the real world. In the summer of 1949, May and I, aged nine and ten, were on the lookout for ways to make cash. Francis Kirwan, the leader of our gang, told us he had earned loads picking strawberries in Donabate. This was our chance. We were going out to pick strawberries. The only trouble was that we needed money to earn money: three shillings for the bus and train fares. We had to ask Mam. She was a cautious woman and didn't share Dad's view that her children should face reality as soon as possible. In fact, she felt nobody should have to face reality if at all possible. She was not impressed when we proposed that she loan us the fare to go out to pick strawberries in Donabate.

'No,' she said. 'I have no money. It's too far. Yis will be killed.'

She was always worrying about us being killed. We cried. We moaned. We sulked. But she wouldn't budge.

As I said, we were desperate. We waylaid Dad at the bus stop. As we walked towards the house, we talked him into giving us the money for our fare. He warned us that it would have to be repaid out of our earnings. Triumphantly, we ran through the front door. 'Dad is giving us the money,' we shouted.

There was what would now be called a 'heated discussion'. Mam said she wouldn't be responsible if we were killed. We had only ourselves to blame.

The next day May and I were standing at the bus stop at 6 a.m., waiting for the 7 a.m. bus. Francis Kirwan had decided not to come. The bus emptied out in O'Connell Street. We pushed through the throng of workers making their way to Amiens Street Station, now known as Connolly Station, where we bought two half-fare return tickets to Donabate. Our train was standing at platform four, hissing steam and belching smoke. Two men, blackened, streaked and sweating, were shovelling coal into the engine. We jumped across what is now known as 'mind-the-gap' into the safety of the railway carriage.

We watched Fairview Park, our last-known landmark, disappear.

May said, 'We might not be taken on.'

Shocked, I asked, 'Why didn't you tell me?'

'Francis Kirwan only told me last night,' she said. 'That's why he didn't come today. He said the big boys are taken on first and loads of kids were sent home last week. The farmer said they were too small.'

We looked at each other across the carriage. Two skinny little young wans in our good cotton dresses and brown sandals. What would we do if we were sent home? Three shillings gone down the drain. Mam would say we had only ourselves to blame. We would never be let out again.

We brightened when we saw the sea sparkling in the sunshine at Malahide.

'Ye never know, we could be taken on,' May said.

The farmer was waiting for us at Donabate Station,

standing beside a large lorry. We saw a queue of big boys in raggedy clothes, with sacks across their shoulders. Perhaps he took pity on us, standing there on tippy toes, so eager in our best, cleanest clothes. He piled us all into the back of his lorry and drove us to the fields. We caught our first sight of strawberry drills, stretching for miles and miles. There were enough strawberries to feed the whole world.

The farmer said we would be paid sixpence for every crate we filled and showed us where to pick. May and I crouched down between the drills and began to attack the strawberries with great ferocity, tossing them in a mangled heap into the crates. The farmer rushed over to us, shouting, 'Stop, stop! Yis are destroying the strawberries.' Everyone was looking at us. We thought we were going to be sent home. But he knelt down beside us and showed us how to twist and pull, then watched us until we got it right. When he left, we stuffed ourselves with strawberries. Juice ran down our chins, staining our hands and good clothes. May was sick and I got the trots. As far as I'm concerned, strawberries are much overrated. Especially Donabate strawberries.

The whistle blew for lunch and I have a vague memory of us sitting on an upturned crate, eating our sandwiches and drinking Oxo out of a mug. We watched the other kids from north Dublin, Whitehall, Cabra and Finglas talking, fighting and playing. May and I were too tired to move.

After lunch, it was back to work. We got into the rhythm of the strawberry-picking. We pushed along the drills on our knees, delicately twisting and plucking, carefully filling our crates with perfect strawberries, wondering when we could go home and how much we would make. At last, the farmer blew his whistle and we lined up to be paid. He counted the number of crates that he had marked in his book. I had earned five shillings and May six. We climbed into his truck and were dropped off in time to catch the train at Donabate Station. On our return journey, we barely had the energy to jump across mind-the-gap. Mam was standing at the hall door waiting for us.

'Thank God yis are safe,' she said. 'Me heart was in me mouth all day. I thought yis would be killed.'

She told us to wash ourselves and leave our filthy clothes steeping in the bath while she made us chips and eggs, our favourite dinner. We handed up our money. Mam said it was enough to buy the dinner for two days. We were earning our keep. She would leave out some old clothes for us for the next day. Dad said he was delighted we had started to earn our keep and he went to the pub for a few pints to celebrate the return of his three shillings.

May and I flopped into bed. We had to be up early the next day. I lay awake, remembering the strawberry beds that went on for ever, the feel of the hard, coarse earth on my knees, the sea shimmering in the sunshine, the money we had made, and wondering if earning my keep was the same thing as facing up to reality.

7

The Wine Coat

Aunt Dolly and Gran brought me to Kelletts on George's Street to buy my confirmation coat. I don't remember them asking me what colour I would like, but I loved the colour they picked: wine. Aunt Dolly said the coat fitted me like a glove and it had better last me a long time, because it was very expensive. Gran didn't say much. Dolly said Gran was beginning to be away with the fairies. They also bought me a wine-coloured hat, which they tested for size by jamming it on my head over my two skinny plaits and pulling the elastic band under my chin to keep it in place.

'I don't like it,' I said. 'It's too tight and too hot.'

'It's lovely on you. It matches your coat. You'll get used to it,' Dolly called, as she went to catch Gran, who was heading towards the door.

My outfit was completed with a beautiful pink chiffon dress. I also got new knickers and a vest, new shoes, gloves and a bag to collect my money.

The night before my confirmation, Aunt Dolly washed my hair and rolled it in rags. Next morning, my beautiful sausage curls wilted within the hour.

My confirmation was a serious affair. The year was 1950. Pope Pius XII had declared it a holy year of special devotion and penance. If you were good, you could earn a plenary indulgence. This was a full of remission of the entire temporal punishment of sin. Imagine! I had no idea what the first part of that meant, but I did get that it was connected with sin. Everything was connected with sin.

On the day of our confirmation, the bishop roamed around the church, pouncing on the boys and girls, asking questions about the catechism, the ten commandments and the precepts of the Church, which we had all learned off by heart. If you didn't get the right answer, you couldn't make your confirmation and would disgrace the whole family. I was greatly relieved to escape without being asked anything.

We also had to 'take the pledge', a prayer that we all repeated after the bishop. I solemnly pledged that I would not drink alcohol until I was at least twenty-five years old.

The ceremony ended with a hymn.

Faith of our fathers, holy faith,
We will be true to thee till death.

We sang with great fervour before escaping from the church out into the spring sunshine.

In the afternoon, Dad brought us to North King Street on the bus to see Gran and Aunt Dolly. Uncle Paddy, who had been demobbed from the army, was there too. I was a bit afraid of him because Gran said he was a bad influence. He was an atheist, which was a mortal sin. He was giving the family a bad name.

We were left in the parlour with him while Aunt Dolly served customers in the shop and Dad brought Gran upstairs to bed. Uncle Paddy asked me, 'Who made the world?' and got me to repeat after him, 'A little piggy with his tail curled,' as he gave me a half-crown for my confirmation. The little piggy with his tail curled was against the first commandment: *I am the Lord thy God ... Thou shalt have no other gods before me.* The half-crown burned a hole in my pocket. Later I told my dad what Uncle Paddy had said.

'Is there really a God?' I asked him. Dad wasn't a bit shocked.

'Don't mind that aul fella. He's not all there,' he reassured me.

Whoever God was, he hadn't stopped Mam from going into hospital again. She had been sent to St Mary's in the

Phoenix Park, which was nearer than Crooksling. This time there was nobody to mind us. Aunt Biddy had gone back to England and Aunt Dolly was busy looking after Gran and the shop.

Dad took in a lodger, Mr Adams, who slept in the parlour on the iron bed Mam had been given by the Health Board. It was covered in grey blankets and a white bedspread. Funny thing, I can only remember that bed in the parlour as if I was looking at it from the ceiling.

Mr Adams was a widower who was sad because he had lost his wife and had no children. He took a shine to me, as Dad said. He had to move out of his lodgings when his wife died and Dad took him in until he found somewhere to stay. I can remember Mr Adams as clear as daylight, his tweed coat, trilby hat and shiny shoes. He was neat and tidy. Mam would have liked that: she was always on at Dad to polish his shoes, to tidy himself up and make himself respectable.

Sometimes Mr Adams brought me to the cinema on Thursdays when he got the labour. One time he had my picture taken by a street photographer on O'Connell Street: a serious little girl in a dark coat with two plaits sticking out from under her hat.

Vague memories of the Carlton Cinema come into my mind even now. The darkness, the walls and a black-and-white film called *Gaslight*, which was about a woman whose husband was trying to drive her mad. Perhaps I saw the film then or later, but I always connect it to my wine confirmation coat.

I had been kept back for a year in school because, with Mam in hospital, I didn't always get my homework done and was absent sometimes. My teacher, Miss Hannafin, said I would be the genius of the year. I thought this was a bad thing because Dad used to say to us, 'You're a right genius,' when we did something stupid. Now I imagine that's what the Christian Brothers used to say to him.

Miss Hannafin was from County Kerry. I knew she loved me. When the inspector came, she put me in the front seat near the window and asked me lots of questions. I loved to listen to her stories about life in Kerry, like the one about the rural electrification scheme when the hens became so confused by the light, they laid twice in one day. She told us about her brother who was a footballer and who played for Kerry in the All-Ireland Final in 1953.

Miss Hannafin was disappointed in me when I stopped doing my homework altogether and became cheeky in class. How could I tell her what was happening at home?

With Mam gone back to hospital, there was nobody to look after us. No one to wash our clothes or make our dinner. When we came home from school, there was nobody there to help us with our homework. Dad had to go to work. Maybe he thought our new lodger might mind us sometimes.

Mr Adams played with us. He taught us to play pitch and toss. Sometimes he gave us pennies when we won. But he was playing other games with me, too. He was putting his hands on me and getting me to touch him. I was having bad dreams and wetting my knickers. My runny ear was oozing and sticky all the time. There was no one to take me to the hospital to have it cleaned out. I felt dirty, smelly and bad.

I couldn't tell Miss Hannafin. I didn't know how to say it to her. I didn't know how to say it to anybody.

I missed my mam and wondered if I would ever see her again. Every Sunday, Dad cycled through the Phoenix Park to see her. May and I used to beg him to take us. He said he couldn't because he wasn't allowed to.

Gran was getting worse. She was taking money out of the till and hiding it, sometimes down her stocking. Chocolate bars too. She was always accusing Aunt Dolly of robbing her blind and giving out to the customers. Things came to a head when she wiped her bottom with a page out of Uncle Paddy's correspondence course. It was part of a chess championship competition, which he was winning. He said Gran would have to go into St Brendan's, the psychiatric hospital.

Aunt Dolly said, 'There is no way my mother is going into "the Union". Everybody comes out of there in a box.' But Gran got so bad that that was where she had to go. When she arrived there, she realised she was in the place where her sister had died. She got such a shock, she went into a coma. Aunt Dolly wanted to take her home to die, so she was brought back to North King Street in an ambulance.

May, Billy and I were brought to see Gran. She was in

the room where we had lived before we moved to Cabra. The curtains were drawn. We could barely see her in the dim candlelight. She was lying on the bed, brown rosary beads wrapped around her fingers. Her eyes were closed and she was making loud noises. Her dry tongue was sticking out. Aunt Dolly was crying and wetting Gran's tongue with a feather dipped in water. The three of us knelt beside the bed and said a Hail Mary with Aunt Dolly. She wanted us to stay and have lemonade and iced biscuits. We just wanted to escape. We ran out of the room, down the stairs and out into the sunlight.

A week later Dad brought me down to North King Street. I said, 'Maybe Gran won't die.' Dad said he knew that she was already dead. The shop was closed. All the neighbours were in the bedroom praying, singing and drinking bottles of stout. Gran was in a coffin. Aunt Dolly kissed Gran and told me to kiss her before they put the lid on. Her forehead felt cold, like the marble on the altar rails. I wanted to run away. Aunt Dolly was very upset. She said it was her fault – that she should never have put Gran into St Brendan's.

On the night of Gran's funeral, Dad and Aunt Dolly were crying. Dad said he should never have been put into the orphanage, that it had ruined his whole life. Then somebody came into the room and he stopped talking. I couldn't believe what I'd heard. When I tried to ask him more about it, he told me to stop bothering him.

After Gran died Dad came into money. He told Mr Adams to leave. I was glad he was gone. It meant that I didn't have to tiptoe past the parlour any more or creep up the stairs to go to the toilet. Sometimes, though, I missed going to the pictures with him.

Aunt Dolly said Dad went a bit off the rails. He got himself a bookie's licence and a backer, a man called Mr Breen, who owned a barber's shop in Dame Street. Dad got a big black bag with DOWDALL printed on the front in red letters on a white background.

Aunt Dolly and I went with him in Mr Breen's car on his first outing to the Tramore Races. We stayed in lodgings in Waterford. The backer's son, Francis, who also came with us, told me he was fourteen. His father gave him the money to take me to the pictures on the first day of the races. I was delighted but Francis was in a sulk. He didn't want to be seen with me in my wine coat on a hot summer's day and no backs to my old shoes because they were getting too small for me. Dad had cut the backs off so I could keep wearing them. I looked like a 'Mary hick'.

Next day Aunt Dolly said, 'Would you look at the cut of that child,' and bought me a new pair of sandals, a cardigan and a dress. I was made up.

Aunt Dolly brought me on a bus through the mountains to a monastery called Mount Melleray. She wanted to pray for Gran and Mam. We prayed for Uncle Paddy as well, because it was an awful thing to be an atheist and he could end up burning in the eternal flames of hell – though sometimes I had heard her wishing Uncle Paddy *would* go to hell because he was tormenting her.

We had our dinner in the monastery and a priest heard Aunt Dolly's confession.

'I had me skillet cleaned. God is good and the devil is not a bad fella either,' she laughed, as we travelled home through the sunlit mountains. She had backed the winner in the last race the day before, at twenty to one. She was on the pig's back.

Dad was delighted when we returned to the lodgings. He and Mr Breen had had a good day at the races and they were in great form, too. The adults went to the pub, and when they got back we all had a sing-song. Dad sang 'The West's Awake'. Dolly sang 'Love's Last Word Is Spoken (Chérie)'. I sang 'Little Boy Blue'. Francis refused to sing and went into a sulk, but his dad sang 'Galway Bay' because he was from the west of Ireland.

Next day, Dad stood on his box in the blazing sunshine, his bookie's bag hanging on the end of the big board. He shouted the odds, took money and changed the prices on the blackboard. Mr Breen gave out the tickets, advising Dad about which horse to give long or short odds on and what bets to lay off, competing against other bookies and the tote.

Francis and I ran around the course spying on the other bookies, taking note of their prices. Most of them employed ticktack men, who made signs to alert them to the ever-changing prices. The punters were moving along the line of bookies, studying form, looking for the best odds. It was by the grace of God I didn't become a gambling addict. The excitement was fierce. Dad calculating the odds, standing on his box, shouting, 'Six to four the field', 'Five to one bar one', wiping the board with a cloth, changing the prices to let out one horse and rein in another. He was red in the face with the excitement and the sun. He was so happy, I thought he might burst.

Then the horses were under starter's orders, on the line, jostling for position, the jockeys trying to keep them steady. The signal was made for the off. The horses' hooves thundered, the crowd cheered. As they approached the finishing line, Aunt Dolly said her heart was in her mouth. Dad started coughing. It looked as if the favourite might win. Then two outsiders surged ahead and Dad calmed down. Aunt Dolly had backed another winner, at twenty-five to one this time.

It was a good day. Mr Breen and Dad shared the profits. I got a half-crown and Francis got ten shillings. The adults had sore heads driving back to Dublin.

The following Sunday we ran after Dad through the Phoenix Park to St Mary's Hospital. Mam came out to see us in her blue pyjamas. She was fat. Her grey eyes were filled with tears as she hugged us. 'You shouldn't be here. You could catch something,' she said.

'I told them not to come but they wouldn't listen to me,' Dad said.

It seemed like a very long time since we had seen our mam. Looking back, it was probably only about six or eight months – a very long time in the life of a child. She was living in a hut with three other ladies. She told us the windows were always kept wide open, even when it was very cold, because fresh air was a cure for tuberculosis.

Shortly after our visit, Dolly told us we had a new brother, Martin. He was called after Blessed Martin de Porres. He was ten pounds in weight, nearly as heavy as a sack of turf. Mam had been transferred to the Rotunda Hospital for the birth. Martin was sent to St James's Hospital in Dublin because there was nobody to mind him. Everybody was upset. St James's was filled with babies who were dying of gastroenteritis, and they were afraid Martin would die too.

Mrs Gaffney, Aunt Dolly's friend, brought me to see Martin. She said he was the most beautiful baby she had ever laid eyes on. He couldn't be left in there to die. Mam gave permission for Mrs Gaffney to take Martin home to her tenement room in North King Street, which was just up the street from Aunt Dolly. She was overjoyed. She had been longing for a baby. Her only child, Phyllis, was twelve years old. She bought Martin a second-hand pram and some new clothes. Phyllis was delighted with her new 'brother'.

The Phoenix Park was covered with a carpet of red-gold leaves when Mam signed herself out again. She had been given a new drug called streptomycin and was feeling much better. She must have walked with her brown case down to Chapelizod to catch the bus into town and got another bus from town to Cabra. She arrived home one Sunday morning. The sun was shining in the kitchen. I was sitting by the fireplace playing with my doll. She hugged me, but gave out about the state of the house. May and Billy heard Mam's voice and ran down the stairs. They threw themselves on top of her.

Dad said, 'Bridie, why didn't you wait until you were better?'

Mam started to cry. She felt well enough to stay at home and wanted her baby, so Martin was brought back. Poor Mrs Gaffney and Phyllis.

We all loved Martin, especially May. She wheeled him everywhere in the big pram that Mrs Gaffney had passed on, alongside the piles of beautiful baby clothes. Our Martin's big brown eyes danced with laughter when May tickled him.

That Christmas, Aunt Dolly came to stay with us. We had a hooley on Christmas Day, but I don't remember much of it. I was sick and lay curled up in Martin's big pram. Mam was afraid I was getting gastroenteritis, but *she* was very well. She cooked the Christmas dinner. Aunt Dolly said Mam looked better than she had in years. Dad had a winner at the races and bought her a new blue coat and navy hat.

In April I was due to have an operation to drain my smelly ear, which would help me to hear better. May minded Martin while Mam and Dad brought me into town to buy me new pyjamas. I got pains in my stomach and vomited just like I had at Christmas. I was brought in a taxi to the Richmond hospital and had an emergency operation for appendicitis.

Aunt Dolly sent me sweets and comics, *The Beano* and *The Dandy*, and a syphon bottle that squirted lemonade. I loved being in an adult ward and listening to their conversations. May minded me when I came out. She thumped Eileen McMahon for calling me 'smelly ear'.

Six weeks later, I was admitted to the Richmond again to have the postponed mastoidectomy on my right ear. The operation lasted for four hours, and I was very sick when I woke up, probably because I had eaten a quarter-pound of bonbons before going down to the theatre. The operation left me with permanently damaged hearing, but I didn't care because my ear had cleared up.

It was decided that I needed convalescence. May was sent with me to keep me company. We went to Mount Merrion Convalescent Home. It was horrible. We missed our home and family. We hated the food and were cold and hungry. We danced for joy when Mam took us home.

Summer came and we were free to roam again. May and I fought over who would push Martin in his pram.

I wore my confirmation coat for another two years. When I finished primary school, Mam bought me a nice respectable fawn coat and my wine coat was passed on to May.

8

Facing Up to Reality

As I came towards the end of my time in primary school, I knew that I wanted to go on with my education. Dad said I could go to secondary school if I got a scholarship. I decided to apply for the Dublin Corporation scholarship. Hundreds of the brightest children from all the best schools were being coached for it. This included a class in my own school. I was at the top of my class in the C stream, but would probably have been at the bottom of the A. The head nun, Sister Mary David, signed my application form. I thought, from the way she looked at me, that she had her doubts.

As it turned out, Sister Mary David was right. The

scholarship was way out of my league. One of the subjects was algebra. I had never even heard of it. Dad said, 'Don't worry. Your uncle Paddy [who was supposed to be a genius] will teach you algebra in a week.' Uncle Paddy declined our request. Teaching me algebra in a week was beyond even his powers. In the end, I didn't fill in the scholarship form. My dad was let off the hook, and I left school at fourteen. Dad never said it outright, but I think he believed education was wasted on women, though he did persuade me to take evening classes in shorthand, typing and English at a local technical college.

It seems strange now that I was wondering about reality as I sat eating my porridge on a bright summer morning in 1953, aged fourteen, on the brink of a great adventure. I was about to set out to look for work with Eileen McMahon, who was also fourteen. My dad's words – face up to reality – invaded my mind like a dark shadow.

Mam's voice interrupted my thoughts. 'Hurry up and finish your porridge or you'll miss the bus. It's going to be a long day. God only knows what could happen.'

Eileen knocked at the door. 'Mind yourselves,' Mam shouted after us as we ran off. We were just in time to catch the number 22 bus at the bottom of Carnlough Road. Oblivious of reality, we stood clinging to the bar of the smoke-filled bus and giggled the whole way into town.

We jumped off at Burgh Quay and surveyed the rows of tenement houses along the River Liffey. They were relics of a bygone age, once the homes of the Dublin rich and middle classes. Now these dilapidated buildings were riddled with small factories making clothes, hats, sacks, soap and many more of life's essentials.

We fought with each other about who would go first. Eileen reluctantly agreed to. Her older twin sisters had told her what to say. Anxiously we mounted the steps of the first house, entered the hallway and studied the noticeboard. The large, higgledy-piggledy building was home to about ten factories. Each floor housed two, and there was a sack factory in the basement. Heading for the dark stairway that led to the cellar, we could smell the outside toilet as we passed through the yard.

In response to Eileen's tentative knock, the door was pulled open by a large, fat woman. 'What do you want?' she barked.

We could see swirls of dust in the sunlight seeping through the basement window. I could taste it in my mouth.

'Any vacancies?' Eileen mumbled.

'No.' The woman closed the door.

On the next landing, we knocked at the first hatch, a garment factory. It was opened by a young girl. 'No vacancies,' she said, shutting the door before Eileen could get a word in edgeways. We combed the whole house. No vacancies. Down the stairs we clattered, out into the light.

'You never asked for the manager,' I said, although I was relieved. I didn't want to work in that dungeon. Was this what my dad meant by reality?

'You'd better go first next time,' Eileen replied.

We had started off that morning in high spirits, taking it in turns to knock on doors and ask for the manager, who was never available. In the late afternoon we sat on the Liffey wall, exhausted, hungry and miserable, watching workers begin to leave the factories.

'We'll never get a job now.' Eileen sighed. 'It's too late.'

'Just one more try,' I said. 'I can't ask for my bus fare again tomorrow.'

'Well, you'd better be the one to ask for the manager,' Eileen grumbled.

Our last go was a hat factory. A man was leaving as we entered the hall.

'We're looking for the manager,' I said.

'That's me.' He smiled.

'Any v-vacancies?' I stammered.

He looked us up and down, our eager faces, our spotless dresses, our short socks. 'How old are you?' he asked.

'Fourteen,' we replied.

'And where do you live?'

'Cabra,' we said. Eileen's sister had told us not to say Cabra West because it had a bad name.

'Your names?' he asked.

'Peggy Dowdall and Eileen McMahon.'

He must have been in a good mood. 'You can start on Monday at half eight. Bring your birth certificates. We'll give you a week's trial. The starting rate is twenty-five shillings a week.'

Eileen and I danced for joy down the quays. We had a job in a hat factory. Twenty-five shillings a week! We could each buy a new bike on the never-never.

On Monday morning we were outside the factory at seven thirty. A nice lady called Rosy, the forewoman, brought us into a huge room filled with sewing machines, bales of cloth, stacks of leather and piles of hats – garda hats, army hats and post-office hats. She introduced us to Anne, and asked her to show us our job. Anne told us that all the workers in the factory were doing a novena for the ending of the war in Korea. We had no idea there was a war in Korea or even where Korea was. But we knelt and said a decade of the rosary for the ending of the war and to stop the spread of communism in the world. The war ended with a truce in July 1953. Perhaps our intercessions were heard.

Eileen and I were given the task of ironing the seams on the lining of the crowns of the hats. Anne, who was barely older than us, showed us what to do. We set to work using four heavy irons, which we heated on three gas rings. We stood ironing those seams and passed them on to the machinists, who urged us to hurry up. They were paid by the dozen and depended on us to keep them going. When we reached the end of one pile, another arrived. It seemed as if we were feeding an insatiable monster. The whir of the machines, the weight of the irons, the hiss of steam, the heat and glow of the gas rings: this was our introduction to the university of work. We had a break at eleven o'clock and an hour for lunch. We sat on the steps outside, eating our banana sandwiches and looking at the sun sparkling on the Liffey. We had another four and a half hours to go.

Two weeks later, I received a letter asking me to come for an interview at I.S. Varian's, a brush factory in Talbot Street, where my dad worked. My parents thought it had better prospects than the hat factory. I passed the interview. Even though I was delighted to be told to start on the following Monday, I was sad that I would no longer be working with Eileen.

I had a bad cough when I started at the brush factory. One of the directors asked me if I had received the result of an X-ray for tuberculosis. It had been taken by a mobile unit that was travelling around all the factories in a drive to eradicate that awful disease. Thankfully, my lungs were clear.

When a vacancy arose at the brush factory for a bookkeeper, a number of us new girls were offered the opportunity to do a maths and English test and apply for the job. An office job was more respectable than a factory job, and it would mean a rise in wages. On the day of the test, I was shaking so much I could hardly write. I had pricked my finger on a nail in the factory and the paper was smudged with blood. Miss Kavanagh, who was supervising, kept asking me questions. I had to guess what she was saying. I didn't want to tell her that, in spite of the ear operation, I was hard of hearing.

'I'll never get that job, Mam. I couldn't hear what Miss Kavanagh was saying.'

'You did your best. God is good. Don't give up hope,' she said.

'Mam! Mam! I got the job!' I shouted, as I wheeled my bike into the hall. 'I'm starting next Monday.'

'That's great. Sure, you were always good at figures.'

'I told you there was no need for you to go to secondary school,' Dad crowed.

I was being trained in by Pauline, who was leaving the following week to get married. Mrs Oglesby, the forewoman, had noticed her thickening waistline. I sat between the two of them behind a large desk, with cushions under my bum to enable me to see over the top – a skinny little creature straining to hear and see in a place called the hair room, where the materials needed to make brushes were stored. Fluorescent lighting bathed the three of us in an eerie glow. Mrs Oglesby sat clicking her false teeth disapprovingly, while Pauline tried to teach me how to weigh the hairs and bristles and enter the numbers in the ledger.

I was trying to master a complicated system of mathematics: addition, subtraction, multiplication and long division. I had to work out whether or not the correct amount of hair had gone into each brush, which included toothbrushes, hairbrushes, bath brushes, paint brushes and artists' brushes. They were all made by machine. The yard brushes were handmade by men who had served a seven-year apprenticeship. They were on piece work.

The senior men expected to be given the best jobs, which paid the most money. Pauline managed them with quiet authority and fairness, ignoring Mrs Oglesby's clicking teeth and crackling nylon overall. They glared at each other while I sat in the middle and bit my nails. I was terrified of the men, terrified of Mrs Oglesby and terrified of losing my job before I had even started.

'Don't worry, Peggy. You'll get the hang of it. Come and see me and let me know how you're getting on,' Pauline whispered. She was an orphan and lived in a room on North King Street, near Aunt Dolly's shop.

Mrs Oglesby must have overheard the conversation. 'Don't have anything to do with that brazen hussy,' she hissed, when Pauline left the room to go to the toilet. Perhaps she was afraid I might be contaminated.

Pauline's wedding was a quiet one conducted on the side altar of Halston Street Chapel. I visited her for a year after the baby was born. She had transformed the tenement room into a cosy nest. I imagined, innocently perhaps, that she and her lovely husband John were blissfully happy. John sat feeding the baby while Pauline cooked me a fry-up. I had never before in my life seen a man feeding a baby.

I remembered a song I heard on the radio at the time:

> *Just Molly and me and baby makes three.*
> *We're happy in my blue heaven.*

I often wondered what became of Pauline, as I desperately tried to step into her shoes.

I might have been good at figures, but I was no use at

giving orders. Mrs Oglesby sat by my side at a desk in the hair room, watching my every move, teeth clicking, pulling her wig over her ears. The more she clicked and pulled, the more nervous I became and the more mistakes I made. Every week she examined the books, while I sat beside her and bit my nails.

After a year, I developed migraine headaches and was sent to have an X-ray. Mam, who always looked on the bright side, feared I might have a brain tumour. Dad said it was because I was up all night dancing and chasing fellas, and 'God knows what will become of you, Peggy.'

Mam was relieved to learn that I hadn't got a brain tumour. She said it was probably my 'others'. She meant my periods, which were a curse anyway. Something terrible could happen to me if I allowed a fella to touch me down there.

'Have respect for yourself,' Mam would say. 'If you don't have respect for yourself, nobody else will. Hold the bone and the dog will follow.' I had no idea what she was talking about. The three words that stuck in my brain were 'respect', 'bone' and 'dog'. Years later, Mam told me that once when she had her others, her dad had brought her, late one night, to Benburb Street, which was near the soldiers' barracks. He showed her the prostitutes and told her that, if she wasn't careful, she could end up like them.

I pictured my mam, a small, sensitive child. Her mother had died of tuberculosis when she was ten, leaving her to the tender mercies of her father. He was a military man, who had been fighting in France when she was born and who was probably suffering from what we now call post-traumatic stress. She never forgave him for having her long plaits cut off the day after her mam's funeral. My mother always seemed to me like a small, wounded bird that I had to mind. I think I absorbed all her pain. My nightmares were filled with women lurking in dark alleyways, dogs and bones, shadows and plaits lying on the floor.

I longed for the happy-ever-after love I read about in books and saw in the films. In pursuit of this dream, every weekend I cycled to all the local dances with my friends, hoping to meet a fella who would bring me to the pictures and ask me to go steady. The first time a boy asked me out, I spent hours doing myself up in the bathroom. Dad couldn't get into his refuge, the only place where he could get a bit of peace: every night he sat on the toilet for two hours reading the paper and contemplating world affairs.

When I finally sneaked down the stairs in my stiletto heels, dirndl skirt, tight black top and see-through plastic raincoat, my mascaraed eyes were beginning to smudge.

'Jesus, Mary and Joseph!' Mam said. 'You mind yourself.'

'Don't you ever take over the bathroom like that again,' Dad shouted.

I barely made the seven o'clock bus and sat worrying would Kevin turn up and if I'd be able to hear him. I was ashamed of being deaf. There he was standing under Clerys' clock, dark-haired, lanky, looking kind of lost.

He said, 'Hello, Peggy. I wondered would you turn up.'

'Well, here I am, Kevin.'

'Would you like to go to the Adelphi to see *Calamity Jane*? We might have to queue.'

Everybody, including me, wanted to see *Calamity Jane*, but I didn't have the money. It was two and six to get in, but when a fella asked you out, he paid. There was no queue. The usherette lit the way to our seats. The air was filled with smoke. The cinema was packed with hundreds of young courting couples. Doris Day played a tomboy who dressed like a man. She wasn't a bit domesticated, but then she fell in love and turned into a beautiful house-trained girl. All my friends longed to be like Doris Day, of secret loves and the Deadwood Stage, whip-cracking away.

I sat in the darkened cinema, transported to the Black Hills of Dakota. Doris Day was singing 'Secret Love' when I felt Kevin's arm sliding over my shoulder onto my chest. I gave him a sharp dig in the ribs with my elbow. That was off limits. A dangerous occasion of sin. Undaunted, he leaned across and kissed me on the lips. I liked it. This was a sin. It came under the heading of impure. Any kind of sexual feeling, I thought, was not having respect for myself. But at least he hadn't stuck his tongue into my mouth. Eileen McMahon said a fella had once done that; it was awful. She fainted outside the confession box. She didn't know how to tell the priest. Her penance was a decade of the rosary.

Romance, books and religion were my main means of escape. I joined the Legion of Mary with my friend Maureen. Looking for guidance, I began to visit the Church of the Most Precious Blood in Cabra West on my way home from work. I hated my job and I hated Mrs Oglesby. I was causing trouble at home, bossing everybody around. Mam said I was a domineering little bitch, a malcontent. Once a month I did a silent retreat in a convent on Merrion Square, thinking I might become a nun. Nothing seemed to improve me. The more I tried to be good, the worse I became. Dad said the road to hell was paved with good intentions. Now I think he was saying that to himself, battling his gambling. I could see no way out.

Mam was struggling with her new baby, Susan, her three-year-old toddler, Martin, and her rebellious teenagers. How she managed to keep the show on the road I will never know. Dad was searching for the next winner, singing 'O'Rafferty's pig was a wonderful animal'. My heart was filled with love songs and my head with worry. Reality was dark and shadowy. The future looked bleak, at the mercy of the next winner, Mrs Oglesby's moods, my mother's health and my own growing sense of the injustice in the world. I wanted to straighten everything out and put an end to all suffering.

I felt trapped. I couldn't leave my job because a steady income was needed at home, even more so as Susan and Martin grew up and started school. I was earning good money and I felt responsible for keeping the family going.

Things came to a head in work. Mrs Oglesby's mission in life, apart from tormenting me, was to rid the country of immorality. She patrolled the factory, reprimanding those she caught loitering, lounging or who were up to no good. My friend Nelly, loud and rebellious, was suspended for a day for singing at the top of her voice, 'I found my thrill on Blueberry Hill,' when she thought Mrs Oglesby had gone.

'"I found my thrill on Blueberry Hill" indeed!' Mrs Oglesby exclaimed. 'And she barely seventeen years of age.' Just a little younger than me.

I sat seething beside her, knowing that Nelly would get into trouble with her family for losing a day's wages.

Seemingly meek and silent, I was the repository of Mrs Oglesby's pronouncements when she returned from her forays. But over the years in the brush factory, I had got braver. I was getting used to working alongside her. One time, it came to her attention that a group of us had bought tickets to see a play called *The Rose Tattoo* at the Pike Theatre. Everybody was talking about it. The whole country was scandalised, even though nobody knew exactly what they were scandalised about. Mrs Oglesby tackled me in front of a few others while I was weighing out bristles for artists' brushes.

'Is it true,' she said, 'that you're going to see that immoral play on in the Pike Theatre?'

'Yes,' I mumbled. There was dead silence.

'Well, I forbid you to go,' she said.

'Mrs Oglesby,' I said, 'I don't have to answer to you for what I do outside of work.'

'I'm responsible for your morals. You are too young to be exposed to such smut. I'm only thinking of your welfare.'

'No, you're not.' I was shaking. I wouldn't let myself cry.

'Are you contradicting me?' she asked incredulously. The others were listening intently.

'Yes,' I said, my pent-up rage spilling out.

Strangely, Mrs Oglesby didn't retaliate.

As it turned out, we didn't get to see *The Rose Tattoo* in the Pike Theatre after all. Included in the script, there had been a stage direction that called for 'a small cellophane-wrapped disk' to fall out of an actor's pocket onto the floor. (Nobody talked about 'condoms' at that time.) Even though this incident had been omitted from the performance, the play was cancelled. The director, Alan Simpson, was arrested and charged with 'presenting, for gain, an indecent and profane performance'. Our morals were safe!

Mrs Oglesby became more patient after our encounter. I think she was finally sensing my struggle. I was way out of my depth, fearful of losing the job I hated while knowing my wages were helping to put food on the table. I was shifted to another job with less responsibility. My headaches stopped. I felt a sense of relief and, at the same time, a bit of a failure. Mam said I was never satisfied.

My true vocation was the pursuit of love. Happy-ever-after love. I wouldn't be satisfied until I'd found it.

9

Pining for Love

My sister May started work at a sewing factory in Capel Street. With the extra money coming in, we invested in a dining-room suite for the kitchen and a chesterfield suite, a coffee-table and a glass case for the parlour. Dad said we were on the pig's back, which gave him some freedom to continue with his main objective in life: gambling. The extra money brought happiness and misery. Dad was away on his magic carpet.

My brother Billy had left school at fourteen and got a job as an apprentice painter and decorator. He started flexing his muscles, gambling and stealing money from gas meters. There was only room in the house for one gambler. Mam tried valiantly to keep the peace and drank large bottles of stout to ease her nerves.

Two years later, Billy ran away to England. At first, Dad said good riddance: it would teach him a lesson. Dad was very strong on teaching lessons, though it took him a very long time to learn one himself. He expected Billy to come crawling back. At home, as we lurched from one crisis to another, I sang 'Secret Love'.

Still yearning for romance, in search of love, I continued to cycle to the local dances with my friends. It was 1957 and we were discovering new music. We learned to jive. May was thrown out of the Carlton Cinema for jiving in the aisle during a rock-and-roll film. She began to dress like a Teddy girl: tight skirt, flat shoes, tight haircut, loads of Pan Stik and black mascara. Mam said she looked cheap and common, and God only knew what would happen to her. It seemed as if the whole family was falling apart.

We were trying to be holy and respectable. I was ashamed of the drinking, the gambling and the chaos in my house. I thought it was somehow my fault. I tried to fix it by bossing my younger siblings and raging against my father, my mother and the world.

Maureen, my best friend, was also the eldest in her family. We were very much in the same boat. Sometimes we walked for miles along the Royal Canal talking about our dreams, mostly of romance. We wanted to escape but we felt responsible for our families.

I was the apple of my father's eye. He confided in me

his hopes and dreams and relied on me as the eldest child to take responsibility for my siblings. He enlisted my help in his search for Billy. Dad said he wanted Billy to have a better life than he'd had. He'd run away himself once, during his time at St Vincent's Orphanage in Glasnevin. This was the first time he'd opened up about the place he'd grown up in, from the age of seven until he turned seventeen. Gran had had no money to keep him and Uncle Paddy at home after their dad died of TB. He said his time at the orphanage was too awful to talk about. He had run away after finding his friend dead in the bed next to him, but he had been found and brought back the next day. There were tears in Dad's eyes as he spoke. He coughed then, as he usually did when he was upset, and said nothing more on the subject.

We wrote to the head office of the Salvation Army in England asking for advice. They traced Billy to Birmingham, where he was living with some lads from Cabra. Some time later we received a letter from him. He had joined the British Army. He had learned to read and write and had been posted to Malaya. Mam was so relieved her darling son was still alive. Billy made her an allowance of one pound, fourteen shillings a week, which helped to keep the roof over our heads.

Mam was pregnant again. She was so ashamed. She kept saying, 'How could this have happened to me at my age?' She was forty-one. She used to carry a towel over her arm to hide her bump.

May and I didn't care. We were in love. May got engaged

to her boyfriend, Brian, before he went to England to join the Royal Air Force. Love hit me like a thunderbolt: my days and nights were filled with the sheer joy and misery of it. Paul – his name sends shivers down my spine to this day. His sister Joan had got him a job in the factory. I wasn't interested in him at first because he was seventeen, a year younger than me. Paul used to talk to me at lunch hour. We were both well read. Aunt Dolly sold second-hand books and our house in Cabra was full of them. I read Dickens, Joyce, Tolstoy, Hemingway, Shakespeare's sonnets and Zane Grey western stories – everything I could lay my hands on. Paul was tall, blond and Protestant. He had a posh accent and stood out like a sore thumb in the factory. He lived with Joan in Walkinstown. Their mother wasn't long dead. I imagine that was why Paul came to work in the factory. It was only a temporary arrangement because Joan was getting married and she and her husband were moving to England.

Such a foolish thing to fall in love. Paul and I were never going to get married and live happily ever after. But love is not sensible. I remember our first kiss, under the big oak tree beside the Royal Canal where I had learned to swim. Such a joyous, tender kiss. The stars exploded in the sky. I was standing on my tippy toes and we just melted into each other. Then Paul went to England with Joan, vowing to write to me.

Every day I watched for the post. A Valentine card arrived with a cave man on the front, carrying a club and dragging a girl behind him. The verse is imprinted on my mind. Surely this was an indication that he loved me:

> *Way back in those cave man days when men*
> *   were mighty tough*
> *A guy could club the girl he loved and treat*
> *   her mighty rough.*
> *But with a girl like you, sweetheart, I'd*
> *   willingly behave.*
> *I'd even throw my club away and be your*
> *   loving slave.*

I heard that Paul had been drowned while training with the RAF in England. Inwardly I mourned him. I thought I was going to die. I had read about people who did die of a broken heart. My Aunt Dolly had been let down years before and never got over it. That was why she always sang, 'Love's Last Word Is Spoken (Chérie)', Mam had told me.

Outwardly, I danced and sang and went out with lots of boys. I persuaded Mam to call our new brother Paul. He was only four and a half pounds in weight when he was born. He brought out the best in us all. So tiny, he slept in a drawer for a few weeks. We poured all our love into him as he grew from a downy little creature into a lively toddler. May's fiancé sent her a turntable and some records. Paul used to stand beside the pickup and say, 'Dance me, dance me,' when we came in from work. We sang along with Frank Sinatra of our high hopes.

My broken heart was mending but I was still pining for love and marriage. May and Brian were saving for their wedding the following year. I was to be bridesmaid and this only whetted my appetite for romance.

In August 1959, Maureen and I spent two glorious weeks in Scotland. We stayed with Maureen's Aunt Mary in her small council house on the outskirts of Glasgow. It was our first trip abroad and we made the most of it. We thought we were hip and knew everything. On our first night out, we clicked with two fellas at a dance. George fancied Maureen and Alex fell madly in love with me, I swear. Aunt Mary was not too happy when we arrived home at one a.m. in a taxi, escorted by two young fellas. She had given us strict instructions to be home by eleven on the last bus.

Alex and George arrived early the next morning to take us into Glasgow to see the sights. We were all done up to the nines.

'Girls, girls, mind yourselves,' Aunt Mary cried after us as we stepped out in our stiletto heels down her garden path. She was relieved when we returned that night, still intact.

'Glasgow is a wild city and young men are only out for what they can get,' she said.

George had tried it on with Maureen. She told him to keep his hands to himself. Maureen and I were good Legion of Mary girls. Sex outside of marriage was a mortal sin, and dangerous.

My Alex was handsome, tanned and interesting. He was studying marine engineering in Stow College and had just returned from a whaling trip in the Antarctic, hence the tan and the money. He was living it up. Alex wined and dined the four of us for two wonderful weeks. When we went to visit Edinburgh Castle, he asked me to marry him. Of course, I said yes.

It was all so romantic, just what I'd dreamed of. I could hardly believe my good fortune. We discussed plans for our future, deciding to have a small wedding in Dublin the following year and then live in Glasgow until Alex finished his degree.

'Be careful,' Maureen pleaded. 'You never know what he might be after. It seems too good to be true.'

Caution was not one of my strong points. I sailed back to Dublin in a hazy glow of romance, announcing as I swept in through the front door, 'I am getting married next year.'

Mam was in the middle of dishing up the dinner. Dad, just home from work, was reclining on the sofa reading the paper. May, Susan, Paul and Martin were sitting at the table with their mouths open.

'Jesus, Mary and Joseph, have I not got enough on me plate,' Mam groaned.

The others burst out laughing.

'And who is this fella?' Dad inquired. 'Where does he come from and what does he do?'

'He is Scotch [as we used to say]. He is training to be a marine engineer in Stow College in Glasgow. He has just come back from a whaling trip in the Antarctic.'

'A sailor!' Dad said sceptically. 'Probably has a girl in every port.'

'Mother of God. What will become of her?' Mam cried. 'I hope nothing happened to you, Peggy.'

'He's not like that. He is a nice, decent, respectable fella and he wants to marry me. When he finishes his exams in September, he is going to come over here to ask Dad for my hand in marriage.'

'We'll see about that,' Dad remarked, casting his eyes to heaven.

Dad was very impressed with Alex, whom he pronounced to be intelligent, well-educated and with good prospects. Over a few jars, Alex asked for my hand in marriage and Dad was delighted to accept on my behalf. Alex was due to go on another trip to the Antarctic in a few weeks and, with the money he would save, we would get married in Dublin the following June.

'He is a decent, honourable man,' Mam said, relieved.

The kids were delighted when we brought them to the zoo and Alex gave them each a five-pound note!

We travelled to Portsmouth to meet Alex's mother, Isobel, and his sister, Carol. Alex bought the ring and we had a celebration dinner, with Isobel and Carol giving us their blessing.

I returned to Dublin betrothed, flashing a three-stone twist engagement ring. I knitted an Aran sweater for Alex and a cardigan for myself. I daydreamed of us wearing them on our honeymoon as I listened to Alex's jazz LPs. We wrote to each other daily. His letters came every two weeks, in bundles, which he posted when he arrived in a port. Oh, the joy when I came home from work and saw the pile of letters waiting on the sideboard. I read them over and over, insisting on reading titbits out loud to anyone who would listen. I sang 'La Mer', one of the latest Bobby Darin songs, at the top of my voice and waited for the next batch of letters from Alex, in my mind sailing, like a bird on high, straight to his heart.

10

A Certain Smile

I was semi-engaged when I met Paddy at a dance in Mills Hall, beside the Shelbourne Hotel. It was April 1960, and this was the first dance I'd been to in months. I felt out of place, wounded and bewildered. I didn't want to be there. My friend Maureen had persuaded me to come to distract me from the shock I had received that day: a bundle of love letters from my fiancé Alex included one that told me he wanted to postpone our wedding, which had been planned for June, just two months away. It had been posted from a port in the Antarctic two weeks before. It seemed my whole life lay in tatters, four days away from my twenty-first birthday.

Paddy kept asking me to dance. While I jived and did slow waltzes, my mind kept wandering to the letter:

Dearest Peggy,

I had a letter from my mam today imploring me to postpone our wedding. She had married in haste. She was pregnant. Just before the war. (I never knew that.) I remember the fights, the silences, the divorce. We had to leave our home and I had to give up my teacher training course. That is why I ended up going to sea. Looking back, I don't think my parents were ever happy. I would not want that for us. I still love you. I am sorry you will get this in between the other letters. We will discuss it when I get back in June.

I felt like the bubble had burst. The future that we had so carefully planned wasn't as fixed as I thought. I was afraid Alex was thinking of calling off our wedding completely. I hadn't told anybody about the letter except Maureen.

Alex's jazz music had filled our small house in Cabra every night, upsetting the kids and setting my dad's nerves on edge. Alex had written to me about all the exotic places he'd visited, places we would go to together.

'We're going to travel the world,' I would announce, showing off my three-stone sapphire engagement ring.

Dad said, 'The sooner the better.'

'I hope it all works out for her,' Mam said.

How was I going to break the news to my family and friends that our wedding was postponed?

Paddy's voice interrupted my thoughts. 'Where do you live?' he asked.

'Cabra.' Usually I said Phibsborough: it was more respectable. But I'd thrown caution to the winds. I wasn't my usual charming, flirtatious self. Paddy told me later he had fallen in love with me on that first encounter. He was a shy man. It must have taken great courage for him to keep asking me to dance.

Maureen said to me, 'That fella is only gorgeous,' after he had asked us would we like a lemonade. He told us he was a postman and lived in Harold's Cross, which was classed as a respectable area.

Maureen said, 'That's funny. My da's a postman. His name is Johnny Byrne.'

'I know him well,' Paddy said.

I can still remember the look in Paddy's eyes as we danced a slow waltz to a Johnny Mathis song, 'A Certain Smile'.

Perhaps I had led an unsuspecting heart on a merry chase. Perhaps I had led many unsuspecting hearts on a merry chase. Maureen always said I was like a magnet for men. I don't know why. I certainly wasn't beautiful. I remember one fella telling me I was attractively ugly.

Paddy was handsome. Intense blue eyes, jet black hair, a neatly trimmed goatee. He was small, neat and immaculately dressed. At the end of the dance, he asked shyly if he could leave us home. Later he told me he couldn't pluck up the courage to ask me out.

Paddy found out about my twenty-first when he was

sorting the letters for Cabra. He sent me flowers. He rang Varian's where I worked. I agreed to go to the pictures with him. (How thoughtless we can be with unsuspecting hearts.)

He met my parents, who loved his quiet acceptance of our mad home. May invited him to her wedding, as though he was part of the family. I didn't know how to tell Paddy about Alex. I felt guilty, deceitful and ashamed.

One week before Alex was due to come to Ireland, I plucked up the courage to tell Paddy. He already knew. Maureen's father had told him. Paddy said he loved me with all his heart and asked me to marry him. Oh my God, the things we do. I kissed Paddy and said I would think about it.

Alex came and stayed in our chaotic home. I agreed to go and live in Scotland so that we could get to know each other better before we were married. Mam and Dad were concerned, but Alex assured them he would keep me safe. He would arrange for me to stay with his friend's fiancée in her apartment.

Paddy didn't seem surprised when I told him I was going to Scotland. He said he would be there for me if I changed my mind. I felt so mean. I only knew that I had to escape from home.

Out of the frying pan into the fire, as Mam used to say.

Things didn't work out quite as expected in Glasgow. Alex and I lost the run of ourselves. I broke my confirmation pledge and lost my virginity. He was living the student life and had lots of money from his whaling trips. He introduced me to all his friends. For a brief time I was the belle of the ball and I loved it.

But underneath I was struggling. Despite the fact that Alex and I were drifting apart, I became pregnant. There was no talk now of marriage. Alex was even reluctant to speak about my pregnancy, but he did think that we should have our baby adopted. I reluctantly agreed. Although I knew that he was legally obliged to provide for me and our child, I was too ashamed to ask. We were bickering all the time. We agreed to take a break while he sat his final exams. Four days later I received a letter in the post.

> *Dear Peggy,*
>
> *I am travelling to Portsmouth to stay with my mother until I go to sea again. I'm sorry to leave you like this. I can't get married. It would be a life of misery for both of us, just like it was for my parents.*
>
> *I know you will manage fine without me. Your Legion of Mary friends will take care of you.*
>
> *I will always love you and remember you with great fondness.*
>
> *Love Alex*

I tried to hold myself together but I couldn't stop myself shaking. Oh my poor heart. Oh my poor child. Oh my poor parents. How would I survive?

But I was blessed. My friends did mind me. I had great joy when my baby was born in a mother-and-baby home in Glasgow, and great sorrow when I gave her away. My broken heart took many years to mend.

When I returned home two years later in disgrace, an unmarried mother minus her baby, Paddy was there to pick up the pieces. It was many years before I could look back over that bleak time of my life and put together the pieces of myself that had fallen apart. Many years before I could grieve the loss of my beautiful baby girl, Marie, whom I'd been forced to put up for adoption. For now, I locked it all away and ran into Paddy's waiting arms and into the safety of marriage, like a bird into a cage. A bad person, determined to be good. Determined to make our marriage work.

In my parents' eyes, Paddy had assumed the status of a saint. How innocent we were. We thought we could make the past go away if we didn't speak about it. We thought doing a pre-marriage course with the Jesuits would prepare us for our lifelong voyage. We had talks on budgeting, home-making and sex.

Sex was the most interesting subject on the pre-marriage course. Sex education was banned in Ireland at that time. A lot of us were practising experiential learning. Sexual intercourse, the Jesuit informed us, was designed for procreation and was a mortal sin outside marriage. I certainly knew this to be true.

'Is it a double mortal sin to have sex outside marriage using contraception?' one guy asked.

Poor Father McCarthy was flummoxed. He had no idea what to say. Divine mysteries were beginning to unravel.

Before the poor man could get his breath back, the impertinent guy asked, 'And what about family planning?'

'The doctor will be here next week to explain about family planning, but I can tell you the Church does allow a certain method of family planning. But only within the holy confines of marriage,' Father McCarthy said, wagging his finger playfully.

'What might that be?' the impertinent guy asked again.

Father McCarthy was embarrassed. 'That's really for the doctor to explain. It's called the rhythm method. It involves tracking the body's natural cycles and having intercourse in the safe period when the woman is least fertile. Even so, every conjugal act must be open to the transmission of life,' Father McCarthy intoned gravely.

Nature being geared towards procreation, this was probably the time when women were least sexy, I thought.

'What about the withdrawal method?' the guy asked. He was beginning to get on Father McCarthy's nerves.

'Wasting the seed is a mortal sin,' the priest said impatiently. 'The doctor will explain all that next week.'

I had already learned about sex and procreation in a very painful way. If dangerous occasions of sin loomed large outside marriage, they seemed to loom even larger inside. With the exception of conjugal rights, of course. Or jungle rights, as they were laughingly referred to.

Will he tell us about hymens, I wondered, remembering when I had told Alex I was pregnant. He had been shocked. 'You can't be,' he said. 'I didn't break anything.'

'Break what?' I asked.

He looked at me incredulously. 'You don't know?' He explained to me about the piece of skin called a hymen, which is intact in virgins. I had read about hymens, but had connected them with kings and queens. I had never connected them to me.

'Are you saying the baby isn't yours? That I've been having sex with somebody else?'

'No, I'm not. I am just saying it's very strange.'

It *was* very strange. I didn't remember anything being broken either.

I wondered now what Paddy was thinking, sitting there holding my hand during the pre-marriage talk. I was painfully aware I wasn't a virgin. Perhaps I had never been a virgin.

'That's been a lot to digest.' Father McCarthy's voice interrupted my thoughts. 'The doctor will explain the details next week.'

'I think we need a drink after that,' Paddy said.

My mind was in turmoil: I was back in Glasgow, three years before. God knew where Paddy's mind was. Yet we sat in the pub discussing the arrangements for our wedding.

We made the most of our courtship. We went to dinner dances, singing pubs, the theatre. We cycled everywhere. We sang calypso songs as we freewheeled through the Phoenix Park – Paddy was a big fan of Harry Belafonte.

We babysat for anybody who asked. It was a way of spending time together, having a snog while the children were asleep, and saving money. We were determined to have our own home and had managed to put a deposit on a house in Marino, our dream location. Still, there was a silent undercurrent of things unspoken. Paddy was jealous and possessive. I thought he was entitled to be that way because of my past.

Sometimes I squashed myself, trying to be who I thought Paddy wanted me to be. I wanted to avoid the awkward silence that would follow if I talked or laughed too much. I was still a gregarious, flirtatious creature. I was also afraid of stepping out of line, though my fear was mostly of my own making. So much lay below the surface of my being. I felt like a sinner who needed to be punished. I wanted to make up for my sins.

We married on a wet St Stephen's Day in 1964. Paddy had booked us into a lovely old hotel beside the River Lee in Cork. It was our first time to stay in a hotel. We arrived late at night. There were two hot-water bottles in the bed. Next morning, the waitress asked how the room was. I said the bed was roasting, and she went into peals of laughter. Paddy was so embarrassed.

Bride was conceived on our honeymoon. Our rhythm method was the joyous sound of the church bells echoing across the river and wasn't very effective! Bride's conception always reminds me of Father Prout's poem:

> With the bells of Shandon
> That sound so grand on
> The pleasant waters of the River Lee.

One week later, we moved into our house in Marino. It was freezing. Paddy attempted to light the range. A pall of black smoke belched out. We had two chairs, a table and a bed. We wrapped ourselves in blankets and wandered from room to room. Jesus, Mary and Joseph, there was only one plug socket in the whole house. A gale-force wind was coming in under the back door, the front door, and through the gaps in the window frames. Paddy went into a state of decline and lay, wrapped in his blanket, shivering on the bed.

'Paddy, you've got this house for a song.' I could hear Paddy's friend Joe Doyle's half-jarred voice in my brain, after the deal was done in the pub across the road from the house. We had signed an agreement on the back of a cigarette carton and had given the vendors a hundred-pound deposit without seeing the inside of the house. Our solicitor later informed us that the agreement was not worth the carton it was written on. He also assured me there was no need for my name to be on the deeds.

When we paid the deposit on the house, it was still occupied by the owner, whose sons were selling it for her. They told us we could see it after their mother had moved out. She was eighty-four and had been a bit doddery since the recent death of her husband. She couldn't live alone, so her daughter had agreed to take her in. The sons didn't want to upset their mother by bringing us to inspect the house before she left.

Were we mad?

Our hearts had been set on Marino, a small estate

designed in the shape of the Tara Brooch. We had walked through Marino for many months admiring the greens, the circles, the tree-lined avenues and the well-kept lawns. Paddy had discovered it when he was delivering the post.

'It's a sound structure. A good investment,' Paddy's friend Joe pointed out, when he came with us to inspect the house for the first time. It was summer. The house was warm and filled with light. We never noticed the gaps in the doors and window frames.

'Original pine floors. Look at how thick the walls are. You'll have the place done up in no time,' Joe said.

All very well if we were handy, but neither of us could put a nail in the wall.

'Peggy, just come to bed,' Paddy moaned from under the blanket. 'We'll talk about it tomorrow. I still have a week off work.'

Things came to a head the next day when I turned on the tap in the bath and the kitchen was flooded. Words were spoken. Paddy went into a sulk. His halo was beginning to tilt.

We were rescued by Paddy's family, who came and did enough work on the house to make it habitable. I discovered that Paddy hated DIY with a passion and was inclined to disappear when things needed to be done. He would be sitting there, waiting for me to cook the dinner, when I cycled home from work, exhausted. I wanted somebody to make my dinner. After all, I was pregnant. Things will improve, I thought, when I have enough stamps to collect my maternity benefit. I could hear Mam's voice ringing in my ears: 'Be grateful for small mercies.'

When I left work, I was lonesome. I missed the singing, the gossip, the laughter, the noise. There I was, sitting pretty with my bump, the silence echoing around the bare house. I watched the procession of hearses go by as the older residents moved on and the skips moved in. The transistor radio was a saving grace. Gay Byrne's voice cut through the silence as I pottered around, wondering how to convert this empty shell into a cosy nest. Most days, I escaped and cycled to Mam's or to my friends' or wandered around town, always coming home in time to have Paddy's dinner on the table when he got back from work.

One morning, as I was leaving the house, my neighbour, who was working in the garden, called, 'Hello.'

'I'm so delighted to meet you,' I gushed. 'I haven't seen any of my neighbours since I moved in.' I propped my bike against the railing and held out my hand enthusiastically. 'My name is Peggy.'

'Mrs Weir-Hart,' she said, extending a limp hand.

'McManus,' I added, as an afterthought. 'But since we're neighbours, what is your first name?'

'Mai. Spelt with an *i*,' she said. 'This is my son, Andrew. Say hello to Mrs McManus.'

'Hello, Mrs McManus,' Andrew said, peeping out from behind his mother. He was about three years old.

'Andrew has nobody to play with. There are no other children on the road.' Mrs Weir-Hart was fully mascaraed, with everything matching. 'The neighbours are all old, and they keep to themselves. I haven't been around much. I've been up and down to Carlow, nursing my mother. She died last year. It was a terrible winter,' she said, in a cultured country accent. 'We never went outside the door.'

Jesus, what joyful news. As well as living in a freezing cold house with a silent husband, I had moved into a dead neighbourhood beside a depressed woman, who insisted on calling herself Mrs Weir-Hart. My poor child was not going to have anyone to play with. Years of misery stretched out before me.

'I'm sorry for your trouble, Mrs Weir-Hart. I have to rush. I have an appointment with the doctor.'

'Should you be cycling?' she asked, looking at my bump.

The exercise must have been good for me because I had an easy labour. I insisted on walking to the Rotunda Hospital. Paddy was terrified I would have the baby in the street. He was relieved to drop me at the door. Fathers were not allowed to attend the birth. Mam was so distraught when I went into labour that Aunt Dolly, a spinster, remarked, 'Now I know how awful it must be to be a mother.' Memories of my first labour in Glasgow came flooding back. Perhaps the same had been happening for my mam.

Our daughter was born twenty hours later, on 8 October 1965, just about respectable. We called her Bride Anne, after her two grandmothers. Paddy fell in love with her when she curled her fingers around his.

At that time, breastfeeding was not encouraged, but I insisted. I just wanted to hold Bride. I was afraid something would happen to her, that something would go wrong. I wanted to take her home. 'Birth number two' was written on the chart above my head for all to see. I was afraid my secret would tumble out by accident. I cried for hours, tears of joy for Bride, tears of sorrow for Marie. Why could I not share my feelings with Paddy? I was afraid to rock the boat. Birth number one had already become an unspoken shadow in our relationship.

There were eight mothers in the ward. We all had our turn of baby blues, sore bums, sore breasts, late nights, early mornings. Breastfeeding was awkward. Babies were supposed to be fed at regular hours to establish good habits. They were suspended in baskets at the end of the beds. You could rock them with your foot when they cried. Some of the babies were cross and the mothers so frazzled that they pushed the baskets too hard. I feared the babies might fly out through the window. We had great fun wondering which one would end up on a passing bus. By now we knew each other's life stories. We felt sorry for the poor women in the private rooms who had nobody to talk to.

The new mothers wanted to rush home, but some of the older women were not so eager to leave the hospital and face the music. Mary, the woman in the bed next to me, was as thin as a rake. She already had ten children. 'Johnny only has to hang his trousers at the end of the bed and I'm pregnant. I couldn't face coming back here next year,' she told us. Dr Browne, the master of the Rotunda – a lovely man – had said she might die if she had any more children, and Johnny was fed up with all the mouths to feed. The doctor waylaid Johnny after the visiting hour and told him of his concern for Mary's health if she had another baby. He suggested the rhythm method as a means of birth control. 'I'd try anything,' Mary said to Johnny.

'Ah, Mary, where would we get a céili band in the middle of the night?'

'Johnny has a great sense of humour,' she told us.

'Don't go to bed until he's asleep,' one woman advised. 'That worked for me for two years. By then I was exhausted, and Willie got very sulky. Anyway, I was dying for a bit meself.'

Various other methods were suggested, including the use of condoms.

'Johnny wouldn't use a condom. He said using condoms was like taking a bath with your clothes on.'

Miriam, the woman across from us, couldn't contain herself. 'Ah, Jaysus,' she roared, 'isn't it a terrible pity about him? You can call on me any time. I have a hammer,' she said, to screams of laughter.

'My Johnny is the best in the world. He just can't keep his mickey in his trousers when he has a few jars.'

That night I lay awake in the semi-darkness, listening to the sounds of the sleeping women and babies, thinking of my mother, who would have had eleven children, had they all survived. I thought of the women sitting up all night waiting for their husbands to go to sleep. The women worrying about missed periods. The women who 'accidentally' fell down the stairs. If all that failed, there were hot mustard baths. Was this love?

What kind of a world was I bringing my child into? I was determined we would have a better life. This would not happen to us. We would have a better understanding. We would live happily ever after, tar-ra-ra-boom-de-ay. Home tomorrow.

'The place is in a bit of a mess,' Paddy apologised, as he turned the key in the front door. 'Joe Doyle and Billy stayed here last night. We had a right few jars. Billy insisted on playing poker.'

This was a quaint old Irish custom called wetting the baby's head. It was almost compulsory for men to celebrate the birth by getting drunk with their friends. Paddy, generally a moderate man, had overindulged.

'I didn't have time to clean up,' he said. 'You know what Joe and Billy are like. They refused to go home. Don't worry, I'll have it cleaned up in no time.'

The watery October sun lit up the black cooker which was covered with grease, the brown-stained sink filled with dishes, the table with empty bottles and overflowing ashtrays. The smell of stale beer and cigarettes completed the joyful scene.

Paddy apologised again while he tried to clean up the

mess. His halo had really tilted now and his wings were tarnished.

'Don't say another word,' I said. 'I just want to go to bed and feed the baby. I'm knackered.'

Paddy rubbed his hand across his forehead. 'Sorry,' he said again. 'I need to tidy the bedroom. We all slept there last night.'

Speechless with rage, I handed Bride to Paddy and got myself ready to feed her. I plopped into the blue leatherette armchair, which Aunt Dolly had given us as a wedding present. Paddy was frantically tipping empty beer bottles and ashtrays into the bin.

I watched Bride lying in the crook of my arm contentedly suckling, oblivious of the chaos. Ah, feck it, I thought. What was the point of being angry? I burped the baby and handed her to Paddy.

'Is she all right?' he asked anxiously, trying to get her to curl her fingers around his again.

'Just perfect,' I replied.

Was this what Mam meant when she talked about putting your nose to the grindstone?

11

Choppy Waters

Paddy and I were battered but we were learning to navigate the choppy waters of marital bliss. Every morning he left home at five thirty to sort and deliver the post. On the way back he collected sticks, then lit the fire and had the breakfast made for me when I got up.

Both of us were determined to make our marriage work, to be the best parents. As the mother, I thought I knew best. I was following the latest guidelines on baby-rearing. 'Let the baby cry; do not feed on demand.' Poor Paddy wanted to lift Bride at the slightest whimper. He was convinced that she would die of starvation or neglect. He listened to her breathing while she slept. We got conflicting advice from all quarters and fought secret underground battles. Mrs Weir-Hart was appalled when I told her I was breastfeeding. 'That's only for cows,' she said. 'It will put your whole body out of shape. It's disgusting.'

I was to be churched as well, a tradition that sat uneasy with many women. Along with being a blessing to give thanks for a successful delivery, it was also a ceremony to cleanse the mother's body of the impurities of childbirth, allowing her to re-enter the church in a 'state of grace'. Even though this ritual was being phased out at the time, many parishes still practised it, laying on another layer of shame.

Funny how you drag your past with you. I was still the eldest daughter, responsible for everything and everybody. Paddy was the youngest child and was used to being minded. I minded everyone with a vengeance, whether they needed it or not. Every day, I journeyed to Cabra with Bride in her new pram, the latest model. It had a lift-off carry cot, which the bus conductor, if he was in a good humour, helped me heave under the stairs, while some kind person held Bride. When I arrived in Cabra, I was done in, collapsing on the sofa to feed Bride before tackling the chaos, as I perceived it to be.

Despite her medication, Mam's health had continued to deteriorate. It was fifteen years since she had left the sanatorium and she was determined to keep fighting. She desperately tried to keep order, staggering around, struggling to catch her breath, while still smoking. She believed brandy, cigarettes and valium were the only things that brought her comfort and kept her going. Dad continued to gamble, spending everything he could lay his hands on, always dreaming of making a fortune. He used to say, 'We'll be flush when my horse comes in.' His favourite song then was:

O'Rafferty's pig was a wonderful animal
Built like a battleship solid and stout.

We often fell off the pig's back and Aunt Dolly always ended up getting us on our feet again, which put Mam into a bad humour. Mam hated to be under a compliment. Dad thought respectability was a terrible imposition and was determined it would never happen to him. Mam yearned for respectability and order, and so did I. I caused murder trying to get them to mend their ways. Lecturing, bullying and cajoling, I fought running battles with Martin, Susan and Paul, my brothers and sister, over housework and homework, being respectable and getting on. Mam used to threaten them with me, saying, 'Just wait till Peggy Dowdall hears about this.' Martin, Susan, Paul and Collywobbles the dog dreaded to see me pulling my pram up the steps. Years later, they regaled each other with tales of my tyranny.

Even as we staggered from crisis to crisis, there was laughter. One day while Dad was eating his dinner, a piece of meat got caught in his throat. I banged and thumped him until he was sick all over the floor. Mam got newspapers, wiped up the vomit and threw the papers onto the fire.

'You're nearly after setting the whole house on fire,' he shouted ungratefully to her, when he got his breath back. 'You're always meddling in something.'

We ignored him and mopped the floor. He was drinking a cup of tea when he discovered that his top denture was missing. He went into a rage and accused Mam of burning his false teeth, the only free thing he ever got from the state. How was he going to work to earn a living to keep his family without his teeth? He had got a new job as a lollipop man. The children adored him, made him cards and knitted him socks and gloves. ('A street angel,' Mam said.) As we listened to his toothless rage, I caught sight of Collywobbles under the television table chewing the teeth.

'There they are,' I said, pointing to the dog. Dad was so delighted, he whipped them out of Collywobbles's mouth and stuck them into his own. Peace was momentarily restored. We held our breath and waited for the next disaster.

Susan was starting secondary school. We had a hooley to celebrate – any excuse for a sing-song. Susan, with all the optimism of youth, sang 'The Lollipop Tree' and we all joined in. Paul danced to see us all so happy. Martin, who was now a teenager and our budding musician, played the guitar.

My dad loved singing and was open to all things modern. He had invested in a television, which had an insatiable appetite and had to be fed with two-shilling coins through a meter on the wall. Dad called television the great domesticator, saying it kept men out of the pub. Mam said it was a pity it didn't keep them out of the bookie's as well. The Beatles bounced onto the screen. Dad thought they were wonderful, a breath of fresh air. His party piece became 'Yesterday' by John Lennon and Paul McCartney, which reflected his state of mind. A shadow was indeed hanging over him. My brother Billy was home, discharged from the British Army having been involved in a car crash in Malaya while drunk. Dad was like a lion that had lost its teeth, and Billy was drinking heavily, terrorising the whole household. I thought it was my moral duty to fix the situation, interfering in my dad's attempts to manage Billy but only making the situation worse. We didn't realise then that Billy was mentally ill.

When I returned from my forays in Cabra, I was not in good nick, banging pots and pans in the kitchen, regaling Paddy with all the gory details while he was trying to eat his dinner. He learned to switch off and stayed switched off for a very long time.

Somehow, we found the energy to have another rhythm-method baby, who was born in 1967. We called him Tomás. He insisted on being fed on demand and slept in our bed. Paddy was not a happy chappy. Not only was I failing in my duties in Cabra, I was also making Paddy miserable. I thought it was my fault, and Paddy agreed.

My mother chided, 'Peggy, you're letting yourself go,' the implication being that Paddy might start looking for somebody else. I was yearning for peace, love and closeness, which I'd thought marriage would bring. Trying to be a good wife, mother, daughter and elder sister, I didn't have time to get close to anybody, not even myself.

Mam had passed on some of her gifts to May and me: her love of cooking, her ability to make delicious meals out of the cheapest ingredients, her lovely voice. She sang even in the midst of trials and tribulations, as she called them. I loved to sing while I cooked. Paddy's money as a postman was little but regular. And he didn't gamble. Although we were poor, I felt secure. I knew how to manage money. Mam's voice rang in my ears: 'Let us be grateful for small mercies.'

Paddy and I were so determined to have a happy marriage, we were afraid to have a row. Instead, there were long, stony silences. Sex was a bone of contention. As I had learned from the women at the Rotunda when I'd had Bride, I'd started to stay downstairs at night until I thought Paddy was asleep. I was exhausted. Paddy was sullen and resentful. Despite all precautions, which included the rhythm method, the withdrawal method, the staying-up-all-night method and Paddy spending long hours studying for promotion, two more babies arrived. Padraig was born in 1971 and Mairead in 1972. We lived with a constant fear of pregnancy. Most of my friends were in the same boat, anxiously awaiting the arrival of their period each month. Of course we loved Padraig and Mairead. Thankfully they were delightful, easy babies. Strangely, even as our family got bigger, there was a certain contentment in the daily rhythm of our lives. We had no time to think.

Paddy and his best friend, John, passed their exams with distinction. They were looking forward to their promotion to clerical officers, which would bring regular hours and a pay rise. That night, we received word that healthy, fit John had died in his sleep. He had never smoked or drunk and walked miles every day delivering the post. He had been part of our lives: he collected Paddy for work every day, studied with Paddy in our house three times a week and gave me lifts to Cabra.

Once again, Paddy went into a decline, this time spending months in bed with all kinds of mysterious illnesses. He couldn't pull himself together. It seemed he had lost the will to live. Thank God it was summertime. Every day I walked along Griffith Avenue, pushing the pram with Mairead at the top, Padraig at the bottom strapped into his seat, and Bride and Tomás holding the handles on either side.

Autumn came. I was shouting at poor Bride and Tomás not to let go of the pram. They wanted to dance in the leaves. I was afraid they might run out on the road and be killed. I worried that Paddy might die. The little bit of money I had squirrelled away was gone.

On the evening Paddy announced that he thought he was going to die, there was a pile of nappies in the bucket, a load of dishes in the sink, and the kids were waiting to be fed. Paddy was worried about what would become of me and the children. 'Worried about me and the kids?' I yelled. 'Don't worry. We'll survive. Haven't we survived for the last six months?'

'Stop screaming. You'll upset the kids.'

'If you're so concerned about the kids, why don't you get out of bed, go downstairs and mind them?'

'Sit down and stop upsetting yourself.'

I couldn't believe my ears. 'Jesus, Mary and Joseph! I can't sit down. The kids are waiting to be fed, there's a pile of delph in the sink and a bundle of nappies in the bucket. You're going to have to pull yourself together. Get help. Do something.'

'I don't know what to do,' Paddy said, slumping against the pillow.

'For a start, get yourself dressed, come downstairs and help me to get the kids ready for bed.' I remembered Mam's favourite expression when she was at the end of her tether. 'Or I won't be responsible for what I do.'

I slammed the bedroom door and marched down the stairs. Mairead was crying for her bottle. Padraig was crying to get out of the playpen. Bride and Tomás were fighting.

I heard Paddy slowly making his way downstairs as I lifted Padraig out of the playpen. 'Dad! Dad!' the kids screeched. They were delighted to see him downstairs.

'Here,' I said. 'You hold Mairead while I heat up her bottle.'

Paddy sat into the armchair and fed Mairead, while I tidied the kitchen and got the tea ready.

The air of desolation lifted somewhat as Paddy slowly emerged from his deep depression. He didn't seek help because we had no idea what was wrong. As winter waned and the trees started to bud, Paddy began to walk along Griffith Avenue with us. We watched Bride and Tomás skipping ahead. They had been Paddy's saviours, giving him something to live for.

And what about us? Paddy was somewhere else, unreachable, treading water. We had survived a storm, managing to stay afloat. I could hear Dad's voice: 'You can sink or swim.' One thing we agreed on: we couldn't manage any more babies. We needed a safe method of contraception. We were lucky. Two fertility guidance clinics had been set up in Dublin, quite near where we lived. This was in defiance of the state and the Catholic Church, which claimed that contraception was immoral and would lead to moral decay in Ireland.

Paddy minded the kids while I got the bus to the clinic. I had to push my way through a group of men and women, who were outside shouting that contraception was murder of the unborn and threatening anybody who entered. My legs were shaking as I climbed the steps and pushed the buzzer. I gave my name and was admitted to the doctor's surgery. The mob was visible from the window behind the doctor's desk. I could hear the chants.

The doctor was nervous as she explained the details of having a coil fitted. It was a fairly painless procedure, which I had not known about. Family planning information booklets were banned by the Irish Censorship Board. Thank God for those brave doctors who set up the clinics to alleviate the suffering of working-class women, who were denied access to information on contraception and had large families they couldn't cope with.

Having the coil fitted eased some of the strain in our marriage. But as Dad used to say, 'God never opens one door, but he closes another.' When I confessed to using contraception, my local priest refused to give me absolution and I couldn't receive communion. This played on my mind. I felt I was a bad example to the children. I heard of a priest in town who was giving out absolution like Smarties. My soul was cleansed. I was starting again with a clean slate and at last I could have a good night's sleep.

12

I Have Something to Say

I stood with my pram at the newly installed pedestrian lights on Griffith Avenue, as I waited to collect Bride and Tomás from school. Padraig was sitting on the pram seat while baby Mairead slept peacefully at the top. I was thinking about how much my life had changed since Bride had started school, just two years ago.

On that day in September 1970, her beaming smile was recorded for posterity by her dad, who had taken her photo as she skipped along the avenue ahead of us, excited to be starting school. Tomás, her baby brother, was trying to wriggle out of the straps of his new push chair, or 'go car' as we called it then. He was a bit of a handful. I was thinking it would be a relief just to have him to mind with Bride now in school.

We could hear the screams of the children as I pushed Tomás along into the school driveway. Bride ran back and gripped the handle of the go car. Parents were not allowed to enter the school building. The children were being taken from their mothers and brought in by the senior girls. Some went quietly. Others were pulled, screaming, from their mothers' arms and were carried into the school, under the supervision of the nuns.

I prised Bride's fingers loose and handed her over to one of the girls. She was crying. I was crying as I watched her disappear through the door. One of the younger nuns put a hand on my arm and said sympathetically, 'Don't worry. She'll be all right.'

Nothing had changed, even in what was supposed to be one of the best schools in Dublin. In fact, it seemed to be worse. At least my mam had been allowed to leave us in the hall and kiss us goodbye. Tears flowed as I walked around our estate pushing Tomás. Determined that Bride's school days would be better than mine, I vowed that I would do my best to change what I could.

Bride's tears had dried when I collected her. Thank God for that.

'It was all right, Mam, but I'm not going back,' she announced.

I thought the road to success and happiness was through education. I was one of those mothers who were determined that their kids would have a good education even if it killed them. To this end I read the *Education Times* every week. Shortly after Bride started school, I saw an ad in the *Irish Times* inviting parents, teachers and representatives of religious orders to a meeting in the Shelbourne Hotel. The purpose was to set up an association that would enable parents and teachers to work together for the benefit of all. Jesus, the Shelbourne. Only rich and famous people went there. What would I wear? What would I say?

For my kids, I would do anything, even brave the Shelbourne. Dressed in my best, I entered a packed room, which was buzzing with the voices of well-spoken and well-dressed people who all seemed to know one another. Conscious of my hearing, I made my way to the front row. Seated at the top table were a teacher, a priest and a parent, all well-known in their field. They had called the meeting to form a committee, which would gather information to present proposals to the Catholic hierarchy. The aim was to have parents elected to the board of management of local schools. The boards were currently chosen by the parish priest and did not always represent the views of the parents.

As far as I was concerned, any person with a tittle of wit could see that dragging children into school by the arms and legs was not a good introduction to learning. Why did the boards of management not know this? As I looked around the room, it also occurred to me that the people who were advocating these changes seemed to be from Dublin's posh southside. And, furthermore, nobody I knew had ever been inside the Shelbourne. Who was going to represent us on this committee? My dad was always talking about class distinction. This was it. Conscious of my accent, my deafness, the dandruff on my collar, I stood up and nervously blurted out, 'This is a wonderful idea. But it is being promoted by middle-class people for middle-class people,' then plopped down on my gilt chair. I had not yet learned the art of subterfuge. To give them their due, they were shocked. This had not occurred to them.

'Would you like to join the committee?' the parent at the top table asked.

Why not? I thought. I had no idea what I was taking on. As my mother used to say, 'Ignorance is bliss.'

I was proposed, seconded and elected on the spot, like a lamb being led to the slaughter.

The committee worked for months putting proposals together to present to parents, teachers and clergy, stating why it was important to have elected parent representatives on school management boards. My task was to organise a meeting for parents in my local parish to discuss our proposals. Mr Crooke, the chairman of the parish council, listened to my request for a room to hold a meeting of parents. He read the leaflets and said he would get back to me as soon as possible. The following week I was amazed to read in the parish newsletter the details I had given to Mr Crooke. He was inviting parents to a meeting, chaired by him, to hear their views. It was to be held in our local church in the room above the sacristy.

On the night of the meeting, I took a seat beside the chairman and the confraternity who were lined up behind a table at the top of the room, on a raised platform, facing the audience. Mr Crooke asked me to remove myself and go and sit with the audience. I took my chair and sat on the platform in front of the parish council. The chairman announced to the packed audience, 'This woman is sitting here because she is hard of hearing.' I couldn't believe it! I had been trying to conceal my deafness for a lifetime. It reminded me of the time in school when somebody had pulled the scarf off Sheila Fish and exposed her bald, scabby head to the whole class.

Legs shaking, voice quivering, I rose. 'I *am* hard of hearing,' I said, 'but I am sitting here because I have something to say.'

The chairman ignored me and attempted to address the audience. Mr Browne, the leader of the church choir and a well-respected member of the community, stood up. 'Let the woman speak,' he said.

The chairman, who was called 'the Monsignor' behind his back, ignored Mr Browne and continued to address the meeting. He wielded the power offloaded to him by the parish priest with a heavy hand. He had upset many people. Innocently, I was slipping into the murky waters of parish politics.

There was a cry from the audience: 'Let the woman speak.'

'Mrs McManus,' the chairman said, 'what have you got to say?'

What had I got to lose? I told them about joining the committee that had been set up to promote educational reform. About my approach to Mr Crooke, believing that he would help me organise this meeting, which was meant to be run by parents for parents. My amazement when I saw Mr Crooke's invitation in the parish newsletter, using the information I had given as though it had come from the Church. I told them about Bride's first day in school, skipping along Griffith Avenue, dying to meet other children, and my horror when she was taken from me by the senior girls and carried into the school crying, 'Mammy, Mammy, don't let them take me.' I told them of my determination that the children of this generation would have a better chance than those of the last.

'Is this true?' Mr Browne asked Monsignor, who was for once at a loss for words. He stumbled and fumbled, huffed and puffed, but couldn't give an adequate explanation.

Parents who had been trying for years to get a hearing from the school management board began to vent their grievances. Their top priority was to replace the outdoor rat-infested toilets, which were used by all the pupils, including children of four and five. Everybody agreed that, in this day and age, a child's first day at school should made not be so traumatic. All the pent-up rage began to spill out.

The Monsignor lost control of the meeting and left. It was reported in the parish newsletter the following week that a group of unruly parents had caused a riot in the parish. That group got together to discuss the issues raised at the meeting. Their priority was to replace the outdoor toilets. They set up a working committee to get in contact with the nuns, who were also eager to have new toilets built.

As well as being the leader of the church choir, Mr Browne was also involved in the wider community. Marino housing estate, which had been built in the 1920s, needed an injection of new energy. The older residents were dying off and a plan for the next generation was necessary. Looking back, I marvel at the skills that emerged from the 'unruly mob' at that parish meeting. The working committee negotiated with the old Marino residents' association and a new chairman, secretary and treasurer were elected. They organised a team to enter the National Community Games, a newly formed event that had come out of the successful Dublin Community Games. Sports and athletic competitions were divided into age-groups and children from around Ireland were encouraged to compete. Throughout the 1970s, this annual event grew and moved from Santry in Dublin to a larger venue in Mosney, Co. Meath.

The Community Games was a starting point for the newly expanded Marino residents' association. As the 1970s rolled on, we organised camogie leagues, athletics, dances for parents; we had chess, table tennis and summer projects. Road leagues were set up and teams from various roads in the area competed against one another on the Marino greens. Paddy was elected assistant treasurer and taught children and adults to play chess.

These years working in the community gave Paddy and me a new focus that we could share with each other as our family grew. It was to become the best time of our lives together. We made so many wonderful friends. Doggedly we continued to press the case for parents to be elected to school management boards. With four children now, it was very important to us that parents would have a say in the running of the school. Eventually this was allowed by the parish church. Our involvement in the community took the weight off our marriage and helped us to stay afloat. Our children were growing up and our lives were busy and fulfilled.

Mam was growing very frail. She was sixty-two years old and, with the help of Streptomycin, had managed to stay out of hospital for over twenty years. When she had the energy, she and I used to go into Moore Street on Saturdays to do our shopping and retire to the ladies-only snug in Madigan's pub. In 1978, one week before Christmas, she asked me to go with her to Kelly's in Thomas Street to buy lino for the kitchen and net curtains. She wanted to have the house nice for Christmas. She could barely walk. I could see she was dying on her feet. We went into the Clock pub. She had a brandy and port to settle her stomach.

My heart was in my mouth as I watched her go off in the bus. Imagine, I never thought of a taxi. At least Dad will have the fire lighting when she gets home and he'll give her a cup of tea, I thought.

Next day, she collapsed and was taken by ambulance to

hospital, where she died on New Year's Eve with all her family around her. What an indomitable, generous spirit she was. I picture her signing herself out of the sanatorium to come home to mind us, not once, but twice. Walking to the bus stop with her cardboard case, determined to live to rear us. We were a wild, ungovernable bunch and she loved us.

She was buried on New Year's Day. I can still hear her saying, 'I will do it or die in the attempt.'

13

The Great Escape

For a while after Mam died, I used to find myself standing under Clerys' clock, expecting her to arrive. Sometimes I would follow small dainty women with nice hats down the street. Still, I was happy that Mam was released from her suffering. Towards the end of her life, every breath she took was laboured, and moving was painful because of her angina. She had ulcers, which made swallowing difficult. Even so, she clung to life like a tiny little bird until, finally, she had to let go. I had spent every waking moment of her last months thinking about her and now I missed her. Dad, aged seventy-three, was stunned after she died. We were all surprised how lost he was without her. He would say, 'Now I can go to the pub anytime I like but it's not the same when there is no one to come home to.' He was lonely and desperate and I was worried because I could not mind him. Our children were getting older and Paddy and I had our hands full.

My sister May came home from England for a holiday the summer after Mam died. She had had three babies by the time she was twenty-two, but she still looked glamorous. She had also managed to go to college and get a diploma in domestic science. Now she worked full-time as a cook in the local hospital. I felt dowdy, dull and worn out beside her, especially when I opened the door and she said, 'Where in the name of God did you get those clothes?'

In earlier years, when our children were small, May and I had been close. Paddy, the kids and I had spent our summer holidays with her in her beautiful Victorian house in Surrey, which she and her husband, Brian, a DIY enthusiast, had restored. We had drifted apart in the last few years of Mam's illness. I loved May dearly and missed her support and our wonderful holidays. Now she was home, and this was a kind of reconciliation.

We were walking down to Fairview Park when we met a woman from Cabra, Doreen Hogan. We hadn't seen her since our schooldays. Although we were no longer girls, we recognised each other. Doreen, like May and thousands of young Irish couples at the time, had emigrated to England when she got married in search of a better life. Now that the tide was turning, she had returned to Ireland to be near her family. She and her husband had bought a big old house in Fairview which was badly in need of repair.

'I had to get myself a job,' she told us. 'The house swallowed all our savings. I used to work in England, so I was glad to be earning my own few bob again. I work for a group of doctors, cleaning houses and helping out when they have dinner parties. Would you like a job?' she asked me. 'I know a few doctors who are looking for cleaners.'

'I don't know,' I said. 'I don't think Paddy would like me to go out to work.'

May was incredulous, shocked. I was the elder sister, bossy when I was young. I had had an office job and earned great money. I was regarded as the clever one in the family.

'What do you mean, Paddy wouldn't like it? What would *you* like?' May asked.

I can still remember the exact spot where I was standing in the sunlight outside Marino Technical College, opposite Fairview Park. I had no idea what I would like. Nobody had ever asked me such a question before. I was shaken. I didn't know what to say. Embarrassed, I said, 'Thanks very much for suggesting the doctors' job, Doreen. I'll call down and let you know next week.'

May looked at me. She didn't have to say a word. I knew what she was thinking.

After May went home, I could hear her voice in my brain asking, 'What would *you* like?' Why had I never asked myself this question? It wasn't only in connection with work; it covered every aspect of my life. May was right about my clothes: I was dressed like a bag lady. Mam had been right: I had let myself go. Above all else, I wanted to be good. I wanted to make amends. I had tried to be what I thought Paddy wanted me to be.

In Ireland at that time, a married woman's place was in the home. Working women, who had a husband to support them, were seen to be taking men's jobs. Men were supposed to be the breadwinners. It was regarded as a slight on your husband if you went out to work. There was also an underlying suspicion about what married women might get up to if they were allowed out to work. They might be exposed to dangerous occasions of sin and lose the run of themselves altogether if they started to earn their own money.

I knew I needed an outlet but I was afraid to broach the subject with Paddy, even though we were struggling to make ends meet. Paddy had to have routine. He had his dinner at one o'clock every day. He hated to be disturbed. Somehow I still felt beholden to him for marrying me. May had given me permission to think about myself. It seemed very selfish.

After days of soul-searching, I decided to bring up the subject when Paddy and I went out for our usual drink on a Thursday night.

'Paddy, I was thinking of going back to work,' I said.

'What? Have you not got enough to do at home?' he said, frowning.

'More than enough,' I answered, 'but we need the money and I want to get out of the house.'

'Out of the house? Why? Are you not happy at home?'

'It's just that I want something more.'

'Something more? What do you mean? I don't know what you're talking about. Where are you going to get a job anyway?'

'A friend of mine said she'd get me a job cleaning doctors' houses.'

'Cleaning doctors' houses? What about our house? What about the kids? Who's going to mind them? You never mentioned this to me. Have you been plotting all this behind my back?'

'No, Paddy. It's just that we need the money and I need to get out of the house, now that the kids are growing up. I'll just be gone while they're at school. I'll be there when they come home. Nobody will be disturbed, I promise you.'

'This has been sprung on me all of a sudden. I'll have to think about it.'

'No, Paddy. I have to let Doreen know tomorrow.'

'You've already made up your mind so. You might as well go ahead.'

Oh, the relief of it. I had no idea how I was going to manage. Still, I would find a way.

14

Labradors

Two pampered labradors bounded to greet me as I hobbled along the tree-lined driveway up to the Moore household. They must have a gardener, I thought. Crocuses, daffodils and all the other flowers whose names I didn't yet know were in bloom in the well-kept borders that surrounded a magnificent lawn. The dogs were scampering around me, barking and trying to jump up on me. Why in the name of God had I worn my best clothes and high heels?

I was wondering what Dr Moore and his wife would be like, and what my duties might be. This was our first meeting. They had taken my friend Doreen's word that I was honest, hard-working and an experienced cleaner. Definitely an experienced cleaner! At home I seemed to spend hours and hours scrubbing floors, doors and windows, tidying, washing and ironing without making any impression.

Organisation, as May told me, was the key. Funny how two people reared in the same house could be so different. My sister was fanatically tidy. All I can say is, I wish I was too. As I mounted the steps, Dr Moore opened the front door. He shook my hand, introduced me to his wife and thanked me for coming.

'I'll leave you ladies to get on with it,' he said, disappearing down the long hall.

Mrs Moore, a tall, casually dressed woman in her seventies, glanced down at my high heels before giving me the grand tour. Six bedrooms, three bathrooms, two drawing rooms, a dining room, a huge kitchen, a utility room and an outdoor toilet. The house was stuffed to the gills with beautiful furniture, antiques and plush carpets. What struck me was the dog hair. On the carpets, cushions, sofas, the wooden floors. Everywhere. I could even taste it. I was wondering how in the name of God I was going to clean all this in three hours.

Mrs Moore said, 'For the moment, just clean the main rooms. Dr Moore and I live alone. We use the master bedroom and bathroom, the kitchen, the dining room, the main drawing room and the utility room, Mrs McManus. I suppose you'd better start in the kitchen,' she said.

It was even worse than mine, and I had four kids. Grease everywhere – on the cooker, the surfaces, pots, pans, floor.

'Your hours are from ten until one. I think Doreen has already told you that the rate is ten pounds per morning. Does that suit you?' she asked, looking straight down at me for the first time.

'That's grand, Mrs Moore,' I said. I didn't know what else to say, so I said, 'It's a beautiful house.'

'This is the broom closet,' she said, pointing to a door beside the outdoor toilet. 'You'll find all the cleaning materials in there. Call me if you need anything else. I'll be in the drawing room.'

For an hour I waged war on the kitchen. At least they had a dishwasher and a washing machine, two of the items I planned to buy when I had saved enough money. I could feel my high heels skidding on the greasy kitchen floor. Flat shoes next time.

When the kitchen was restored to some semblance of order, I had to tackle the dog hair. This was not helped by the playful labradors, Melissa and Vanessa, who skidded across the clean kitchen floor with mucky paws, wanting me to play with them. Madam called from the drawing room, 'Girls, girls, stop annoying the cleaning lady.' They paid not one blind bit of notice of her and followed me through to the drawing room, which Mrs Moore had vacated, while I made a valiant attempt to hoover up the hair. My good skirt and jumper were covered with it. I was itchy all over and I still had to tackle the master bedroom. I got a terrible turn against labradors. At least Mrs Moore had told me not to touch the bed. At one o'clock, she inspected what I had been able to manage and paid me my ten pounds.

I staggered home in my high heels, feeling my ten pounds in my pocket. I was thankful that I had tidied our kitchen and made the dinner before I left home.

So, that's how some of the other half live, I thought, as I made a cup of tea and collapsed into a chair. Isolated in a big empty house they can't manage. I could smell the loneliness. I lay on the chair until the kids came home from school. They threw their bags and coats on the floor and shouted, 'Mam, Mam, what's for dinner?' At least it was made. Only another few weeks and I'd be able to buy a washing machine. The kids were going to have to help me.

It would be nice to say they all started to pick up their clothes and wash the dishes and that Paddy started to cooperate, but sullen resistance was the order of the day. I conducted running battles with Paddy and the kids about housework, homework and gardening. The kids thought I had turned into a monster (which I had), and Paddy kept saying, 'Why you don't give up that bloody job?'

On top of all that, Mrs Moore never seemed happy with my work. Admittedly, housework was not my forte. To my surprise, I was learning on the job. So what if there was dust on the top of the dresser? Definitely pernickety,

I told myself when she instructed me to wash down the walls of the three bathrooms. I took refuge in the outdoor toilet. I was fuming. My skirmishes at home had taught me a thing or two. Who does she think she is? I stayed in the back toilet for a good forty minutes while Mrs Moore, Melissa and Vanessa wandered around the house looking for me. When I heard them in the hall, I flushed the chain and emerged.

'Oh, there you are,' Mrs Moore called. 'We were wondering what happened to you, weren't we, girls?'

'STOP!' I shouted at the dogs, as they jumped up on me. 'STOP!'

Mrs Moore was clearly shocked. The dogs sank silently by her side.

'Mrs Moore,' I said, looking up at her. 'I need to speak to you.'

'What's the matter?'

'I'm sorry, Mrs Moore,' I said firmly, 'but I will not be scrubbing down the walls in the three bathrooms. Nor will I be cleaning the carpets in the bedrooms. You need to get contract cleaners in for that.'

I was as startled as she was.

She peered down at me in astonishment. 'Oh, Mrs McManus. I'll have to discuss this with Dr Moore. I don't know what he'll say to that,' she said, shaking her head.

'Let me know next week,' I replied. She took a ten-pound note from her pocket and handed it to me.

Mrs Moore stood at the front door, watching as I

sauntered down the drive, Vanessa and Melissa trotting beside me. I patted their heads and they licked my hands as I walked through the front gate. I went back the following week and Mrs Moore and I parted ways by mutual consent.

15

All Different, All Equal

Around the time Mam died, Bride was beginning to assert herself. Suddenly she was a teenager and Tomás was following closely on her heels. They were a force to be reckoned with. There were heated discussions about secondary schools. Bride refused point blank to go to the local Catholic secondary school, or to Marino Technical College. She had her heart set on going to Mount Temple, which was nearby and offered the promise of more freedom. It was a comprehensive interdenominational school for boys and girls; they were not required to wear a uniform. It was very different from other local schools. Tomás backed her up, saying he wanted to go there as well. They were a formidable team.

They had heard all about Mount Temple from their friends Seamus and Niamh, the children of our close friends Joe and Vera, who were delighted to recommend Mount Temple. They advised us to go to the open day, which was the following week. If we were happy, we could put Bride and Tomás's names on the waiting list.

Although I had walked by the school, pushing my pram, for many years, I had never paid it much attention. As far as I knew, it was a posh private boarding school for boys. What a surprise when Bride, Tomás and I went through the gates, walked past the lodge and entered the vast grounds of the Mount Temple campus. The first thing that caught my eye was the headmaster's gracious old house, surrounded by modern arts blocks and science labs. There were libraries, a huge gym, vast hockey and rugby pitches, and tennis courts. What a revelation! I thought of Marino Tech, squashed in between a row of shops in Fairview. Bride and Tomás were in their element. Niamh and Seamus gave them a conducted tour and introduced them to all their friends. This was the school for them.

As it transpired, all our children went to Mount Temple and have always said that it was one of their best life experiences, despite difficult transitions from a strict Catholic education to a liberal Protestant one. (At first they went a bit wild and lost the run of themselves.) They have maintained friendships with people from all classes and creeds. The same is true for me.

While Bride and Tomás were savouring the delights of Mount Temple, I wandered into the school café, where the parents' association was dispensing refreshments and information. As I sat sipping my tea, I was joined by a tall lady who asked politely, 'May I join you?'

'Of course,' I replied.

'My name is Jennifer. I'm in the parents' association,' she said, extending her hand.

'I'm Peggy. My kids brought me here. They're hell bent on coming to this school. They want me to enrol them. I wasn't sure, but now I'm impressed. I had no idea what was beyond the gates that I pass every day.'

Jennifer gave a brief history of the school and encouraged me to join the parents' association, if my children gained admission to the school, as she put it. Little did I know that becoming involved in the Mount Temple parents' association would have such a profound effect on my life. It gave me a glimpse into another way of seeing the world, another way of living.

Educationally, Ireland had been on the march since the 1960s, when free secondary education had been introduced for all. There was a desire for change. Parents had begun to establish Educate Together schools themselves. Previously a private boarding school for Protestant boys, Mount Temple School had reopened in 1972 to provide state-funded second-level education for the Protestant population of north Dublin. Then the board had agreed to open its doors to girls and pupils of other denominations to get access to state funding. I suppose this fitted with the motto of Mount Temple: 'All different. All equal. Without the Lord, it is in vain.'

When I volunteered to go on the parents' association committee, my motives were not entirely altruistic. I wanted to know what kind of school, and what kind of people, I was exposing Bride to. The parents were mainly middle-class, liberal-minded Protestants, who had consciously opted for this educational experiment. I met Edna, who lived in Sutton but was originally from County Clare. She and I were the only two Catholics who volunteered to go on the association's committee. Edna's husband, Gavin, was a headmaster in a Catholic school, but they had decided they wanted their children to have a more liberal education and to be exposed to a broader social mix. We were welcomed with open arms. Mount Temple was an experiment: in a class- and gender-divided Ireland, education was used to keep people in their places.

The parents' association ran well-organised committee meetings. Edna and I agreed to set up a parent roster to run the school library. We were given the names and addresses of all the first-year pupils. We were to call to their houses and ask the parents if they would like to help. Edna was one of the warmest, most loving and intelligent people I have ever met. I can still hear her soft Clare accent. Both of us had four schoolgoing children. I also had a part-time job. There was not much time to spare but we allowed nothing to interfere with our three mornings a week, when Edna and I would set off in her yellow Mini on a great adventure.

We started at the top of Howth Hill and worked our way down. Most of the parents were delighted to welcome us into their homes. Edna and I each put on a half-stone, they plied us with so much food. They opened their hearts to us and in turn we opened ours to them. Some had sent their children to Mount Temple for financial reasons: they could no longer afford the fees for private schools. Others had sent their children for social reasons: they wanted them to move beyond the Protestant and Catholic enclaves. Some parents were worried that the school's reputation might be dragged down by the influx of poorer pupils from different backgrounds. Many were concerned about gender mixing. What might happen to their daughters, who would now be exposed to rampant teenage boys? But most were willing to give it a try.

We discovered that the Mount Temple parents had the same hopes and fears for their children, whether they were rich or poor, Protestant, Catholic or dissenter. The difference was that poor, uneducated parents didn't have the means. Large families were mainly Catholic. Protestants had a better way of regulating theirs. It was clear they were not using the rhythm method. We met one Protestant family who had eight children.

'Do they not know they're Protestants?' Edna said to me.

We had many discussions about education, religion and class. Edna and I were soulmates, although we came from different backgrounds and had had different life experiences. We shared an aspiration for a more equal society. Edna had lived on a small farm in County Clare and, despite being poor, all her siblings had a good academic education. Rural people saw education as a means of escaping poverty. On the other hand, coming from Cabra, I knew only one girl who had gone to secondary school. Marie Long was known as the girl who went to college. She was kind of excluded. She had moved out of our league.

Edna had come to live in Dublin when she was eighteen. Somebody had got her a flat in Rathmines. She arrived on a Friday and stayed in the flat until Monday morning, when she got the bus the wrong way out of town. She finally arrived, late for work, in the offices of Dublin Corporation, with her brown cloth scapular outside her jumper. Most people kept them hidden from sight. The only instruction her parents had given her when she was leaving home was to wear it at all times to protect her from harm; to go to Mass every week; and always to wear clean knickers in case she got knocked down. She roared laughing when she thought of herself being introduced to her boss with her scapular hanging outside her jumper.

Edna described the class structures in the country. They were even more deeply entrenched than in Dublin. Small farmers, big farmers, doctors, solicitors, publicans, shopkeepers, priests. Woe betide the person who attempted to move outside their own circle. Coming to Dublin had given Edna much more freedom. I suppose she and I were hippies at heart, trying to escape the constraints of our parents' generation, trying to create a better world for our children. We were also searching for a spiritual path.

We were part of a small stream of fellow travellers,

heading for a broader river, cautiously dipping our toes into the water and finding our own level. Despite my splendid aspirations, I was not as open as I thought I was. Jennifer, whom I had met on the open day, offered to drive me home one evening. She was tall, auburn-haired, well-dressed and very posh. Feeling a bit intimidated, I politely refused, saying, 'I live just across the road. I can walk home.' She insisted. I felt too embarrassed to refuse again. She drove me home just across the road. I felt very uncomfortable and wondered why she had picked on me. She parked her car outside my front door. I don't know why I felt so awkward. I just wanted to escape.

'The library project seems to be going very well,' Jennifer said.

'Yes, it's great. People are willing to help.'

Out of the blue, she said to me, 'I think you're wonderful.'

What does she mean? I wondered. The cheek of her. Who does she think she is, patronising me? I was genuinely bemused. 'What are you talking about?' I asked. Nobody in the whole world had ever said that to me, not even Paddy.

'I just admire the way yourself and Edna got the library project set up.'

I didn't know what to say.

'Thanks for the lift home,' I said, opening the car door before Jennifer could say anything else.

'See you next month,' she called cheerily.

'Thanks,' I mumbled, and stumbled out.

Edna and I both felt intimidated by Jennifer. Neither of us had ever met anybody like her. We discussed her in great detail: her accent, her hair, the way she dressed, her commanding presence. Despite our efforts to brush her off, Jennifer seemed determined to get to know us. She was no shrinking violet. We declined her offer to join us as we continued to visit the parents on our list. We had moved down from Howth, Sutton and Portmarnock, and were now visiting the poorer areas of Coolock, Donnycarney and Artane. Such an amazing variety of people. We recruited lots of volunteers to work in the school library.

Jennifer continued to drive me home from the committee meetings. I was too polite to refuse and, in spite of myself, I was beginning to like her. She lived on the Hill of Howth and felt isolated and marooned there. Confined to mixing in a certain circle, she longed to know how the other half lived. Just like me, Jennifer had no money of her own. She had set up a cooking co-op to earn some. Despite appearances, we were in the same boat.

Pope John Paul II came to Dublin in 1979. Edna drove me and the kids to the Phoenix Park in her Mini. Jennifer was dying to know all about the visit. Edna wondered why Jennifer was so interested in the pope. After all, she was Church of Ireland. Edna was a devout Catholic and went to her parish church every day.

One morning, the parish priest approached Edna as she was leaving the church. 'Mrs Ryan', he said. 'The very woman I've been looking for. I've been watching you, and I have something special to offer you.'

Edna said she got the fright of her life.

'I was afraid he was going to ask me to clean the church,' she said. 'As you well know, chaos reigns supreme in my house. If Gavin heard I was going to clean the church, that would be the last straw.'

I knew how she felt. I don't think we envisaged cleaning the church as part of our spiritual journey.

Instead, Father Marky asked her would she like to join Opus Dei. Much worse than cleaning the church.

'Gavin will go mad,' Edna said. 'Rightly or wrongly, he thinks that Opus Dei is a secretive, right-wing and elite institution. The total opposite of the ethos of Mount Temple.'

The priest was so enthusiastic that he wouldn't take no for an answer. 'Go home and discuss it with your husband. I'm sure he'll be delighted.'

'On no account are you to join that fascist organisation,' Gavin shouted. 'I'll have something to say about that.'

At the same time, Jennifer asked us to join a counselling course, which she was starting in her house in September. Edna was very upset. 'Why would I join a counselling group with Jennifer Wilson? Have I not got enough problems of my own? As for Opus Dei, Gavin is threatening to take on the parish priest himself.'

One morning Edna announced, her face beaming, 'I'm pregnant. Thank God. I won't have to join Opus Dei or Jennifer's counselling course. I will have my hands full enough with a new baby.'

I was shocked. Edna was forty-one. 'That was a very

drastic way to avoid the counselling and Opus Dei. Could you not have just said no?'

She gave me one of her looks.

'By the way,' I asked. 'Were you using the rhythm method on top of the piano?' Gavin was a classical pianist and had two grand pianos in their small three-bedroomed house. They had to squeeze past one to get into bed. The two of us got a fit of laughing.

Gavin took great delight in telling the parish priest that his wife would not be joining Opus Dei because she was pregnant. A perfect excuse, as far as the priest was concerned. 'How wonderful,' he said. 'Take her home, get her to put her feet up and make her some soup.'

'I don't believe you,' I said. 'Did Gavin get you to put up your feet and make you the soup?'

'He roared laughing all the way home and said, "What century is that man living in?" He went back to work. I put my feet up and had a cup of tea.'

Jennifer said, 'No problem,' when Edna told her she wouldn't be going to the counselling.

'Peggy, are you still coming?' Jennifer asked me.

'I don't have a lift,' I countered, somewhat relieved.

'Don't worry about that. I have a friend who'll pick you up.' Jennifer was very persistent.

'What does this counselling involve?' I asked.

'It involves learning listening skills. When people are listened to without interruption or advice, they find their own answers to their own problems. I've found it helpful in my own life.'

It didn't sound too bad. I suppose I was curious.

'How much time will it take?' I asked. Paddy was already complaining about Edna and me gallivanting all over the place in her Mini, the state of the house and the kids being neglected.

'One morning a week for ten weeks and occasionally we run weekend residential workshops,' Jennifer said.

I knew there was no way Paddy would agree to that, but I said to myself, 'I'll cross that bridge when I come to it.'

I was disappointed Edna couldn't join me on this new adventure. I would miss her moral support but I wanted to dip my toe in this river.

I went home, cleaned the house from top to bottom, cooked Paddy his favourite dinner, egg and chips, and made myself presentable.

'What's all this about?' Paddy asked suspiciously, glancing at the spotless kitchen and smelling the chips.

'Sit down and eat your dinner before it gets cold. Oh, by the way, I have something to tell you.'

16

A Bumpy Ride

I wondered what I was letting myself in for as I hung out the clothes on that September morning in 1979. I could smell the subtle autumn change in the air. 'What am I searching for?' I mused, as I tidied the house while waiting for Jennifer's friend, Polly, to collect me and bring me to the counselling class in Jennifer's house on the Hill of Howth. My nerves were at me, as my mother used to say.

Polly arrived exactly on time, nine forty-five. She was tall and leggy, dressed in a quirky hippie style. Her smile lit up her whole face. She had lovely teeth.

'Hello, Peggy,' she said, stretching out her hand. 'I'm Polly, your driver for today.'

'Thanks, Polly,' I said. 'To tell you the truth, I'm a bit nervous.'

'Perfectly understandable,' she replied, in her posh English accent, as we slid into her two-seater open-topped sports car. My hair was standing on end as we zoomed up the hill and arrived at Jennifer's house twenty minutes early.

Jennifer brought us into the kitchen and made us a cup of tea. She was glad we were early. It gave her time to fill me in while we waited for the others to arrive. The group I was joining was called 're-evaluation counselling', which was new to Ireland. It had been started in America by a man called Harvey Jackins. Jennifer explained that the course was based on experiential learning and peer assessment. I had no idea what she was talking about.

Jennifer went to answer the doorbell. Polly, seeing the puzzled look on my face, put a hand on my arm and said, 'Peggy, I've been in this group for two years now and I've survived. The most important lesson you have to learn is how to listen, to yourself and others.'

'Listening,' Polly went on earnestly, 'is a most miraculous thing. It can transform your life. It certainly transformed mine. The course is not easy. It can be a bumpy ride. But hang in there, Peggy. You'll get all the help you need.'

Well, I thought, I've just survived one bumpy ride. My hair is standing on end and my heart is thumping, but I'm still in one piece.

'We're all here,' Jennifer called from the drawing room. 'Come and sit beside me, Peggy.'

Jennifer's drawing room was comfortably shabby, filled with nautical trophies. Through the window, I could see ships streaming across a sunlit Dublin Bay. As I sat in the circle, I studied seven well-dressed women and one man. Jaysus, if Paddy ever finds out there's a man in the group, I'll never hear the end of it, I thought.

Jennifer asked each member to stand and introduce themselves, then say what they would like to gain from the group. Some of them were experienced counsellors, glad to be back after the summer break. They seemed to express themselves with great ease. When my turn came, I could hardly remember my own name and I had completely forgotten theirs. I found it hard to hear in groups. I managed to stand and blurt out, 'My name is Peggy McManus and I would like to gain confidence,' and plop back onto my chair. I was consoled when the other newcomers seemed equally nervous.

Jennifer confirmed that the course would run on Monday mornings for ten weeks. 'There are a few ground rules, the most important being confidentiality. Are you all agreed with that?' she asked. Everybody said yes. 'Confidentiality is a sacred contract we must make with one another in order to provide a safe place for us to work,' she said.

God, this is beginning to sound like Opus Dei, I thought.

I hardly heard the other ground rules. My mind was still grappling with the sacred rule of confidentiality. I had no problem keeping a confidence, but I was wondering what I might reveal of myself.

Jennifer then asked us to turn to our neighbour and practise listening skills with them. We had five minutes each. She would call time. Thankfully, my neighbour Audrey spoke first. I thought she was very brave. I knew immediately what Jennifer meant when she said, 'Listen without giving advice or interrupting.' I thought I definitely knew the answer to Audrey's problem. I wanted to tell her to stop crying, she was only upsetting herself. I also wanted to give her some advice about what she should do, but I managed to keep my mouth shut.

Jennifer called time and it was my turn. I didn't feel so bad after hearing Audrey's story. I told her that my legs were shaking. I had never been in a group like this before. I was hard of hearing and had missed some of Jennifer's instructions. I was too embarrassed to ask Jennifer to speak up. People think you're stupid if you tell them you're hard of hearing. Audrey never said a word and, in the silence, I told her I was worried that Paddy would find out there was a man in the group. Two secrets had slipped out in five minutes: my deafness, which I'd managed to conceal for most of my life by lip-reading or figuring out what was being said, and my continuous worrying about Paddy.

'Time,' Jennifer called, and we turned back to the group.

I wanted to hug Audrey for being so kind.

Jennifer asked us what we had learned from the exercise. I had discovered the importance of confidentiality. I felt privileged that Audrey had trusted me enough to reveal herself.

Audrey said she felt safe to tell me what she was struggling with. Jennifer asked her would she like to work in the group. Audrey agreed. Jennifer sat beside her and took her hand. Audrey started to cry again. She sobbed her heart out, deep, racking sobs. I wanted to cry with her. I could feel the tears welling. I thought of my mam and my heart went out to the whole world.

Audrey's story was one of betrayal. As it unfolded, her sobs began to subside. She became calmer. Then she gave a sigh of relief and stopped crying. Jennifer asked Audrey was there anything else she wanted to say. Audrey said, 'No, I'm much better now.' She looked around the room and smiled at us. I could hardly believe the transformation. Jennifer explained that crying was the natural release of grief. Often when we are allowed to release the feelings, we can re-evaluate the situation. I thought of Bride on her first day at school, sobbing her heart out. She had skipped out of school when I collected her.

Polly volunteered to go next. Something came up from her childhood. I saw a bruised and battered little girl beneath the radiant smile and I thought how little we know of anybody. I knew what Polly meant when she said listening was a miraculous thing. In her case, it was literally a life-saver. I understood now what Jennifer had meant by experiential learning. I couldn't wait to practise it on poor Paddy.

Jennifer then asked us to take a few minutes to reflect on what we had learned and to share it with the group. Kindness was the word that came to me. There were so many other words – love, acceptance – but deep down I was afraid of what might surface if I stayed with the course.

'Polly, please don't drive so fast,' I implored, as I slid into the car.

'Oh, Peggy, I'm so sorry. Why didn't you say sooner?'

My head was in a spin as Polly drove along the coast road back to my house. I felt tired, fearful, but elated. So many strong feelings had surfaced as I listened to Audrey and Polly. Mam would have been appalled by how much they had revealed in the group. We had spent our lives making sure our secrets never slipped out. I could hear Mam's voice in my brain: 'Don't tell anyone I have TB. Never tell anyone your business.'

'Are you okay?' Polly asked, interrupting my thoughts as she stopped the car outside my house.

'I'm just a bit shook. I'll be all right when I get a cup of tea,' I replied.

'Are you sure?' Polly asked, touching my arm.

'Yes. I'm all right.' I wanted to get into the house and be by myself. So many things were bubbling up. I needed to cry alone.

A lump of grief was in my throat. Mam had died only a year before. I had tried to mind her but, in the end, I was relieved when she'd died. I felt so guilty for that. Mam had had a lot of pain in her life and, in my heart of hearts, I was glad she was at peace. I thought of Dad as a little boy in the orphanage, hungry, frightened, unloved, and how often we ignored him when he tried to tell us about his life, as he sometimes did in dribs and drabs when he had drink taken. But he never again mentioned the death of his friend. Oh, his poor heart. Now he was living alone, desperate and miserable, with all the freedom in the world and missing his 'life's sparring partner', as he used to call Mam. I was haunted by so many things. I cried for the whole rotten, stinking world.

Eventually I splashed cold water on my face and combed my hair.

'Mam, what's for dinner?' Mairead shouted through the letterbox, just as I had done with my own mother.

Later I listened to the kids fighting and chattering as I cleared away the dishes. As they begged to go out and play, I shouted, 'You have to do your homework first!'

Mam used to say, 'My mind is a hell to me.' Because I was hard of hearing, I heard her say, 'My mind is a health to me.' I was glad she had a healthy mind because her body was so sick. Now I knew what she'd meant. She must have worried about everything. That was what drove her to drink, I thought. Sometimes my mind was a hell to me. I was trying to keep the best side out for the kids' sakes.

Paddy was also struggling. The job he had studied for years to get had not turned out to be the panacea he had imagined. Would we all survive another bumpy ride? Still, I knew in my bones there had to be something more to life. Polly's radiant smile came to mind.

Perhaps Jennifer had seen my struggle and known I

needed help. She was the guardian angel who accompanied Paddy and me on that bumpy ride for the next few years. We became lifelong friends.

We never know what we'll unearth when we go digging deep in the underworld. Sometimes I cursed Jennifer for enticing me to go on that journey. I felt as if I was digging in a quarry with a teaspoon. My life was upended. I did a lot of crying. I was not easy to live with. Nonetheless, I managed to hang in for the ten weeks, clearing small spaces. I was learning to listen and beginning to understand that I was not in charge of the whole world.

I was also accompanied on my journey by fellow travellers who were kind and loving and gave of themselves so willingly. We healed ourselves and each other. None of us were experts. Counselling was not regulated at the time, but there was rigorous peer review and evaluation. Between classes, we had individual sessions. An experienced counsellor worked with a beginner. These sessions were a lifeline for me.

There were strict guidelines. We did not give advice. The theory was that everyone had within themselves the solution to their own problem. Each session would last an hour. The time was equally divided, which meant we had to put aside our own problems and listen to the other person. We learned to use the time constructively, to take responsibility for our own feelings and behaviour. There was no fee. People gave freely of themselves. When you see another human being stripped of their pretensions, you cannot but love them.

Naturally, once again, I thought I could change the

world. Old habits die hard. The first person I wanted to change was Paddy. One night, we were out for a drink. I decided to listen, instead of my usual talking to fill the silence. We looked at each other for about five minutes. Not a word was spoken. Eventually, Paddy asked, 'Is something wrong?'

'No, I'm okay,' I said. I had to sit on myself to stay quiet, hoping that Paddy might say something.

After another few minutes of uncomfortable silence, he remarked, 'Do you know? I never realised we had so little in common.' Imagine, all I had to do was stop talking for this to occur to Paddy.

I learned about patterns of behaviour. I could see who was dramatising and who was stuck. I knew what they needed to do. Sometimes I managed to keep my mouth shut. I tried to practise my counselling skills on everybody, without much success. My best friend fell out with me when I tried to introduce counselling into our complaining sessions. We usually spent our time giving out about our husbands and our miseries, which meant that, in counselling terms, we were rehearsing a pattern. When Nora stopped giving out, I asked, in my best counselling sympathetic voice, 'Is there something you like about John? Is there something you're looking forward to?' She looked at me as if I was mad.

Then I was telling her a story about Mam and I started to cry. She said, 'For God's sake, don't be upsetting yourself. Isn't she better off gone? That counselling is bad for you. Give it up.' Despite my best efforts, I was grieved when Nora and I drifted apart.

Polly's radiant smile, Jennifer's encouragement and the support of the group kept me going. Something about Polly's emotional wounds and her recovery gave me the courage to persevere. Hope springs eternal. I thought I could heal the hurt and rifts in our family. I thought if we could begin to speak to each other openly and honestly we could all be transformed and love each other. Such innocence. I had forgiven myself. Now I was breaking the unwritten rule in our family: 'Whatever you say, say nothing.' Silence was the way we had survived. My efforts were treated with polite but hostile resistance. I knew I was causing upheaval, blundering in where angels feared to tread. I had to re-evaluate the situation and back off.

Even though I felt I was stirring up a lot of muck, I was also clearing small spaces, experiencing tiny moments of peace. Although my path seemed to be littered with obstacles, I was determined to continue.

'Thank God that's over,' Paddy remarked, at the end of the ten weeks.

'Paddy, I'm really sorry for upsetting everybody,' I said, 'but I have to continue.'

'Jesus, if this keeps up, I'll have to go to counselling myself.'

'That might not be a bad idea,' I replied. I could have asked in my nice counselling voice, 'And what would you like to talk about?' but I knew him better. Instead, I announced tentatively, 'Paddy, there's a residential workshop coming up.'

17

A Secret Never to Be Told

I'd been in the counselling group for a year and was beginning to think I had 'emerged'. This was the term used to describe persons who had liberated themselves of their conditioning and were able to live in the world like a free spirit. Ha! In essence it meant I was not so fearful or sad and I was beginning to care for myself.

I was feeling a bit cocky when Polly called in her sports car one rainy Friday evening to take me to a weekend workshop on sexuality in All Hallows College in Drumcondra. I had previously attended workshops there on class and racism. The most important for me was the workshop on class, where I learned to take pride in being working class.

Darkness was falling as I slid confidently out of Polly's sports car. I could hear the call of the rooks as they flew home to roost in huge dark trees that stood in the grounds of the college. A poem I had learned in childhood kept running through my mind:

'Caw!' says the rook as he flies overhead.
It's time little people were going to bed.

I shivered as if somebody had walked across my grave. Polly, ever mindful, touched me and asked, 'Are you okay, Peggy?' as we climbed the steps and entered the large imposing hall at All Hallows. Jennifer, my dear friend, was sitting inside the door behind a table with a tiny woman, whom she introduced as Gabrielle. They were welcoming, registering and collecting fees for the workshop from those who could afford to pay.

We were doing our own catering to keep costs down. My contribution was a vegetarian lasagne, the first I had ever made. I hoped it tasted as nice as it looked. I had put in garlic and lentils and made a tomato sauce using the recipe I had learned on a government-funded catering course I was attending with AnCO. Jennifer had offered me a job in her catering business, but I had needed some training. I was delighted now to able to pay with my own money.

All in all, I was feeling fairly okay when Polly and I took our places in the packed conference hall. Diane Balzer, an American woman of colour, was leading the workshop.

She was tall, with curly black hair cascading down her back. She was sassy, as my favourite poet, Maya Angelou, would say. She had worked all over Europe and America, running workshops on women's liberation and sexuality. She was gung-ho about women's sexual oppression, which I had never heard of. She would have scared the living daylights out of Paddy and the other men I knew.

We were asked to introduce ourselves and say what we expected to gain from the workshop. I said I wasn't sure. I just wanted to learn. Small workshops were set up and leaders were assigned for the next day. This exercise took up most of the evening. We finished with a sing-song. I sang 'Once I Had a Secret Love', the song I used to sing when I was fourteen. For some reason, it made me sad.

Polly asked me how I was as we drove home. I said I was tired but looking forward to the next day. I had signed up for a workshop she was running because I felt comfortable with her.

Paddy was delighted to see me home in one piece and made me a cup of tea. We went to bed early. Both of us had an early start. Paddy was playing pitch and putt the next day, and my course was starting at 8 a.m. sharp. I was looking forward to it.

Saturday was grey, windy and wet. Not a great day for Paddy's pitch and putt. I was glad I had made a coddle for him for when he got home later. Polly seemed a bit preoccupied when she picked me up at seven thirty. 'How are you?' I asked, as we zipped up wild and windy Griffith Avenue.

'I'm a bit nervous. This is my first time to lead a workshop on sexuality. I don't like to stir things up again.'

I remembered the poor broken little girl I had seen on the first day. My face must have told a tale.

'Don't worry, Peggy. I'm okay. I just needed to say it out loud,' she shouted, as we ran from the car park in the pouring rain.

The workshop opened with a song, 'Morning Has Broken', which I loved. We all joined in, singing from the sheet music that had been provided. What a joyful way to start, I thought. I'm going to be all right.

We were asked to turn to the person on our left, break into pairs and take five minutes each to introduce ourselves. We were to notice how we were feeling, to listen and to allow each other to voice any expectations or fears. My partner's name was Carol. She was small, round and young. With her grey-green eyes looking anxious, she blurted out, 'I'm gay. This is my first workshop.'

I was a bit shocked. I had never met anyone who openly confessed to being gay. I hoped my face didn't betray my reaction. Once again, I was struck by how powerful silent listening can be. Carol told me about her childhood, spent in a small town in the west of Ireland, fearful that people would find out she was gay, especially her parents.

'Oh, Peggy,' she said, when her time was up. 'That is the first time I ever told anybody.'

Having listened to Carol's description of her childhood in Castlebar, trying to hide her secret, I could feel myself shaking. My secret tumbled out. 'Carol,' I said, 'I had my first baby adopted twenty years ago.'

Carol's eyes were filled with concern as she watched me shaking. She put her arm around me. Remembering my first workshop, I said, 'Don't worry, I'll be all right.'

'Time,' the leader called. 'We have a half-hour break for refreshments. Workshops begin at eleven sharp.'

Carol and I had a cup of tea and went to our separate workshops. Carol's was on gay and lesbian issues. My workshop, on early sexual memories, was taking place in room eight. Polly had arranged nine chairs in a circle with song sheets and notes for the workshop. After we had introduced ourselves, Polly opened with a song. We stood up and did the actions, sticking out our tongues, making awful faces, like I did when I was about seven, and sang:

> *Nobody loves me, everybody hates me*
> *They all say I eat worms*
> *Long thin slimy ones*
> *Short fat fuzzy ones*
> *Gooey, gooey, gooey, gooey worms.*

My shakes stopped. We broke into threes to talk about our earliest sexual memories, one listener, one observer and one talker, ten minutes each. I was the observer as Mairead described her earliest memory to Margo of sitting in the bath looking at her brother's 'mickey'. I could see the look of surprise on Margo's face. 'My mother told me it was called a penis,' she informed Mairead. (Margo was English.) Then Margo told me about her mother sitting her down and telling her the facts of life, which she found very shocking. She thought it was dirty.

I remembered watching my mother washing herself. I wanted to see what the lumps under her blouse looked like. She exposed one breast, washed it carefully, dried it and put some talcum powder under her arm. I could see the hairs and her nipples. Now I think it was a sacred moment; it remains like a painting in my mind. Then Mam noticed me. 'Peggy Dowdall, what are you looking at? Can I not have a bit of peace? Go out and play.'

Polly called time. We reported what we had learned as a listener, talker and observer. As a talker, I had gained a sacred moment with my mam. As an observer, I had seen the shock on Mairead's face when Margo corrected her and knocked her off course. Listening to Margo, I thought, There is no exact right way to tell your children about the birds and the bees.

Lunch was a blessed relief. My task was to fill the water jugs and set the table, which was a great distraction from my whirling thoughts.

Back in room eight, Polly opened with another song 'We're off to see the Wizard'. We spent the rest of the afternoon uncovering childhood memories and myths. We all remembered playing spin the bottle, doctors and nurses, and kiss chase. I recalled running for miles, but nobody wanted to kiss me. We shared the tall tales we had heard explaining where babies came from. I had thought the doctor brought them in his black bag. Someone else had thought they came out of her mother's belly button.

Margo might have been dismayed to hear the facts of life, but most of us were bewildered. We had no idea what was happening to us when our breasts began to sprout and stick out through our school uniforms. Some began to walk with a hump, pulling their breasts in to hide them, and were further embarrassed when told to straighten up and stop slouching. To add to our misfortunes, we got our periods. Some were told this was a present from Our Lady. They were now young women and must have respect for themselves. They were not to be seen flaunting themselves, getting a bad name and bringing disgrace on the family. In my case, as well as being told to hold the bone and the dog would follow, I was warned not to come home if I got into trouble.

It was such a relief to share our common experiences. Most of us had spent our teenage years bewitched and bothered, walking a fine line between flirting and modesty, afraid of being too forward or not forward enough. We found out the facts of life through trial and error. Room eight rocked with laughter as we described trying to hang on to the bone, sailing too close to the wind, losing the bone and the dog running off licking his chops. There were also tears. Sometimes the price of losing your bone was high. We sang:

> *Come all ye maidens young and fair,*
> *And you who are blooming in your prime.*
> *Always beware and keep your garden fair,*
> *Let no man steal away your thyme.*

On that note Polly announced a half-hour break.

Outside, the sun was shining. I felt the warmth on my face as I sat on a bench under the window of room eight, listening to a robin singing. I felt I'd lived a lifetime between leaving home that grey windy morning and the sunlit afternoon. Nothing remains the same, I thought.

> *Humpty Dumpty sat on a wall*
> *Humpty Dumpty had a great fall*
> *All the king's horses and all the king's men*
> *Couldn't put Humpty together again.*

The nursery rhyme kept running through my mind as I took my place beside Margo in the circle in room eight.

Polly said that after all our hard work on dogs and bones we might as well start with a popular song, and we sung '(How Much Is) That Doggie in the Window'.

Margo volunteered to work with Polly on something that had been triggered for her when Mairead had mentioned seeing her brother's mickey in the bath. All the information her mother had given about the facts of life was of no help to Margo as her elder brother had abused her from the age of ten until she was fourteen. Pleas to her mother fell on deaf ears. Her mother told her to wrap herself up in a sleeping bag and she would be all right. Margo became so disruptive that her parents sent her to a boarding school. It was a shock to see the beautiful, tall, red-haired, sophisticated Margo crumble before my eyes. As people worked in front of the group, I realised no one was there by accident. Long-buried secrets rose to the surface to be revealed and healed. I felt sick to the pit of my stomach, shaking and gagging. Polly worked with me, but no memories surfaced.

Jennifer, Polly's support person, asked Polly would she like to take some time to work with the group. Delicately, lovingly, silently Jennifer created a space where Polly could choose to revisit memories of the prolonged sexual abuse that had crippled her young life. Once again, Polly's anguish triggered something in me. I could feel my heart thumping. I started to bite my nails, which I'd done when I was little. I feared Polly wouldn't be able to come back from that place, but she was in safe hands. Jennifer was a gifted counsellor. Gradually Polly's tears subsided, and she looked around the room. Jennifer asked Polly to describe the classroom. She asked her to breathe and feel her feet on the floor. As Polly gazed around the room, her smile returned.

Jennifer looked her in the eye and said, 'Polly, you know how impertinent I am.'

'Never,' Polly replied. 'What is it you want?'

'Do you think you could muster up a good memory?'

I thought this was going beyond the beyonds, as my

mother used to say. Amazingly, Polly remembered a song her mother used to sing to her, 'Whispering Hope'. Strange, we used to sing it when we'd sat in Mam's bedroom thirty years before. It was one of my dad's favourites. Polly started to hum it and I joined in:

> *Soft as the voice of an angel*
> *Breathing a lesson unheard*
> *Hope with a gentle persuasion*
> *Whispers her comforting word.*
> *Wait till the darkness is over,*
> *Wait till the tempest is done,*
> *Hope for the sunshine tomorrow*
> *After the shower is gone.*

Jennifer explained how easy it is to get trapped in old or frightening emotions when exploring memories of the past, and how important it is to have a focus in the present to return to. I knew this to be true, but I could feel myself slipping into a dark place. Something was bubbling in the pit of my stomach but I didn't know what.

The Angelus bell chimed. It was time for dinner. The dining room was filled with the clatter of knives and forks, the buzz of conversation and noisy laughter. I could see Polly talking animatedly to Diane Balzer and I wondered how she could be so normal.

Will I survive? I wondered afterwards, as I cleared the tables and washed the dishes in the kitchen.

Back in the conference hall, I took my place in the front row beside Polly. Diane Balzer was facilitating feedback from the workshops. All had gone well. We finished with a question-and-answer session and set out the timetable for Sunday.

We ended with another of my favourite songs, 'Kumbaya':

> Someone's singing Lord, kumbaya.
> Someone's crying Lord, kumbaya.
> Someone's healing Lord, kumbaya.
> Oh Lord, kumbaya.

Jennifer drove me home. Polly was staying behind to do some work with Diane. We were too tired to talk in the car.

Paddy's pitch and putt had been a bit of a disaster in the high wind, but he had heated the dinner for the kids and the kitchen was nice and clean. He had also bought a baby Powers to make me a hot toddy to drink while we were watching *The Late Late Show*. I just wanted to collapse into bed.

'You look tired, Peggy. How did it go?' Paddy asked.

'Good, good. We had great fun,' I lied. 'Too much singing, that's what has me knackered. I'm going to bed after *The Late Late*. I want to be up early tomorrow.' Why could I not say a word to Paddy about how I was feeling? My stomach was churning. I took myself off to bed as soon as I could. Strangely, I fell asleep. I didn't even feel Paddy getting into the bed.

I woke about four with an awful pain in my neck. I felt paralysed and trapped. There was an image of eyes staring at me. There was something in my mouth. I wanted to cry out but I didn't want to wake Paddy, who was snoring. Sliding out of the bed, I managed to crawl to the bathroom and was sick. The dawn was breaking as I gathered my clothes and crept downstairs. I lay on the sofa waiting for Polly. My heart was thumping, my body shaking. Images of unseeing, staring eyes kept flashing through my mind. Hands and unspeakable images. I must be a bad person. Please, God, help me.

Stiff with cold and fear, I stumbled into Polly's car.

'What's wrong?' she asked.

'Oh, Polly. I've been up most of the night. I woke with an awful pain in my neck and terrible, terrible images. I can't stop shaking.'

Polly put her arm around me. 'Well, Peggy,' she said, 'it may sound a bit mad. Your shaking is a release of fear. I know it feels awful, but this is a good sign. Allow yourself to have a good shake. As long as your legs don't fall off before we get to All Hallows, we'll be okay.'

The cheek of her, I thought.

'Peggy,' she said, cutting through my fear, 'I want you to breathe. Feel your feet on the floor and give me directions to All Hallows.'

We arrived half an hour early. Jennifer and her friend Gabrielle met us at the door. I could hardly stand up.

Polly, Jennifer and Gabrielle ushered me into an empty classroom. I slumped into a chair and cried and shook while they held me.

They were repeating, 'Peggy, Peggy, keep your eyes open. Look out at the sky. You are safe now. No one can harm you.'

There were no words, only fragments, images and terror. The shame was like sludge. Even thinking about it made me feel dirty, bad and ugly. Eventually my shaking subsided. I looked up at the three calm faces gazing back at me. I felt strangely peaceful and so grateful. I felt loved, loving and trusting, probably for the first time in my life. It was but a fleeting glimpse.

With the help of those skilled healers, I stopped blaming myself and turned it outwards. I raged against God and the whole world. This process lasted a few years. I was too ashamed to tell Paddy, afraid he wouldn't believe what I was struggling to believe myself. Despite my best efforts, I was furtive and unpredictable. Paddy began to think I was having an affair. I realised that, despite all my talking, I was always afraid to reveal myself. I felt so unlovable, afraid that if Paddy really knew me, he wouldn't love me. How little we know of ourselves and each other. Yet, somehow, we survived through prayer, divine grace and willingness to stay the course.

Rage emerged when I shone a light into the darkness. I flew out of the cage I had locked myself into and embarked on the next leg of my journey, as my dad would have said. Once again, I was trying to save the world with even more enthusiasm. I trained as a counsellor and group facilitator. Jennifer and I set up community development groups all over Dublin, running personal development, assertiveness and sexuality courses.

18

I Am Somebody

One evening in 1982 I stood in the packed church in Seán McDermott Street with Paddy and our children, then aged between ten and seventeen, listening to Jesse Jackson. He who would be selected as the Democratic candidate for the American presidency two years later. He was speaking to and conversing with the local community of Dublin North Inner City, telling them that peace, joy, love and forgiveness were possible even in this world. Hundreds of schoolchildren listened in rapt attention as he told of his childhood in America, about the poverty he had endured, and discrimination because he was African American. His mother was only sixteen when he was born. Jackson's harsh upbringing had made him determined to help make this world a better place. He had worked his way through technical school and college and had got a scholarship to university. He had become a Baptist minister. Now he was working as a political activist all over the world.

'If I can, you can,' he told the audience.

Jesse Jackson was like an exotic bird that had flown across the seas into the church. A tall, handsome man of immense passion, singing a song of freedom. He had a wonderful voice and led the congregation in song. The church reverberated with the sound of:

> We shall overcome.
> We shall overcome.
> Deep in my heart, I do believe
> We shall overcome some day.

'And with this faith,' he said, 'we will go out and adjourn the counsels of despair and bring new light into the dark chambers of pessimism. We will be able to rise from the fatigue of despair to the buoyancy of hope.' 'We Shall Overcome' was being sung on the American civil-rights marches, and on marches all over the world for peace and justice. I felt I was connected to a vast movement, surging on a wave of love. For a moment time stood still. We were united in a common cause. I was overjoyed that Paddy and the kids were there with me.

Jesse asked the children to stand. He told them that each child was important. No matter how they spoke or where they came from, they were precious. Their contribution to the world was important. Then he asked them to place their hands on their hearts and say, 'I am somebody,' then turn to their neighbour and say, 'You are somebody.' This went completely against the grain for most Irish people, never mind the residents of the North Inner City, but they shouted the phrase until the church seemed filled with joy. How Jackson managed it, I do not know.

I wondered how I might have responded if, as a child in my own church, I had heard those words. Then I remembered my confirmation. The fear of being picked on by the bishop and asked a question, even though I had learned the Ten Commandments and the Six Precepts off by heart. I would have been too frightened to answer.

I thought of my dad, who had mellowed with age. He was now in his seventies. He had taken such a long time to learn that he was somebody. Now, at the age of forty-three, I had blossomed because of my counselling experience, which had come from America. I could say to myself, 'I am somebody.' And say to my children, 'You are somebody.' When I was a child, to say that would have seemed like boasting and I would have been told off.

Jesse Jackson spoke about love in simple language. He was full of fun. He said, 'Love yourself. Make peace with yourself. Forgive yourself. Take pride in yourself and your community.'

It was just like the lessons I was learning in counselling, as I slowly healed past wounds.

The next speaker was Seán McBride. Bishop Desmond Tutu had also been invited to speak but the South African government would not allow him to leave the country. Seán McBride was a Nobel Peace Prize winner, aged seventy-eight. At the time I thought he was very old. He had a strange French accent, which somehow made his voice sound hypnotic.

He was born in Paris in 1904 and lived there until the age of twelve. Following the execution of his father by a British Army firing squad for his part in the Easter Rising of 1916, Seán was brought back to be educated in Ireland. He lied about his age and at fifteen became involved in the Irish Republican Army (IRA) and took part in the War of Independence. He was imprisoned during the Civil War. He was arrested again later on suspicion of having been one of the assassins of Kevin O'Higgins, the minister for justice in the Free State government in 1927.

McBride had been involved with the IRA in a violent campaign against the state. He had a rather murky past. Now here he was in Seán McDermott Street church, talking to his audience about peace and justice. What a journey he had travelled. Bishop Desmond Tutu, Seán McBride's revered friend, had sent a message to us: 'No man is beyond redemption.' I dearly wanted to believe this, but sometimes I found it hard. McBride spoke eloquently about the need for peace and justice, citing South Africa's apartheid policy as a flagrant breach of human rights.

I was in my element. I had found my niche. I was in that church, at that time, because I was working for the North

City Centre Community Action Project (NCCCAP), which was hosting the event. Once again, a guardian angel had come along. As I said earlier, I had joined an AnCO course, which was run by this group, to develop catering skills so I could work in Jennifer's catering co-op. Moira Smyth was my training officer. We got on well together. She could see that my counselling experience would be helpful to her. She knew I was currently running personal-development courses at Marino Technical College. The vocational educational committees were also beginning to broaden their curriculum and I was working in lots of vocational schools around the city.

Moira asked me to apply for a job as a personal development trainer. I was interviewed by the AnCO team, which included Moira and a member from the project management board. I got the job, ten hours a week. I was in the system and paying PRSI (Pay-Related Social Insurance), which gave me an independence that boosted my confidence no end.

At that time AnCO was the national training authority and had been set up to encourage change within companies, to get them to accept training and development as a means of becoming more competitive. They also provided training in local communities. Many forward-thinking, innovative people were involved. AnCO had funded and supported the NCCCAP. They had set up a board of management, which included lawyers, employers and locals, to evaluate the needs of the community.

The group included Tony Gregory, the popular local

Independent deputy in the Dáil. He was a great role model for the inner-city community, a tireless worker and a private, modest man. Everybody knew Tony was Somebody.

In consultation with the local community, training courses were set up to provide alternative education for young boys and girls who were dropping out of school because they didn't fit into the education system. They were vulnerable to drugs and crime. The board had organised catering, sports and photography courses, which were running well. On Moira's advice, they now planned to introduce personal development courses. I was in the right place at the right time. The work I had done on classism, racism and sexism in the counselling group had given me a head start on other candidates.

Learning the theory was all very well, but the work I had done on myself was more important. The shame I felt about where I had lived when I was growing up, the shame of poverty and alcoholism, had given me some understanding. Thank God for my inexperience, though. I had no idea what I was letting myself in for. I ended up learning a lot more than I taught. These were tough, streetwise kids. I was neither tough nor streetwise. Moira provided the toughness, and I provided a space where the kids could give out about Moira. I was the saint and Moira was the sinner. We worked very well together, but it was still an uphill battle.

Most of our pupils had been damaged by an education system that didn't work for them. Unemployment was rife in the inner city: hence the need for these training initiatives. The students needed to learn by doing practical, useful things. Moira ran the cookery course. She got great results. Her pupils, mostly girls, learned budgeting, cooking and hygiene skills. They built up their self-esteem and their confidence by achieving small tasks, such as planning a meal and buying the ingredients, preparing and cooking, setting the table and serving the food. We cooked and served hundreds of lunches for the workers in the building where we were training.

I also got a job with the accountancy firm Haughey Boland & Co., one of Jennifer's clients. She provided executive lunches for the board. Once again, I saw how the other half lived, but only for a short time. I was good at working in the kitchen, but I was no use waiting on tables because of my shaky hand, which I'd had for many years. My hearing problem didn't help either. Jennifer had to deliver the news that my services were no longer required. All the work I had done in counselling helped me to deal with the shame of being sacked.

I had also left my good cleaning job with Mrs Moore and her labradors. Not quite the same thing as being sacked, but I was beginning to rise above my station in all respects. I was not very popular at home either. I was becoming so busy at work, I was often missing from the house. Even counselling had not helped me to achieve bilocation!

I was very passionate about counselling. I thought it could solve every problem under the sun. My real skill, though, was teaching personal development. The courses were run on a wing and a prayer. Every group had different needs. I tried to design each course around the specific needs of the individual group. The slagging was sometimes merciless. God only knows how we survived the role-playing. Sometimes I had such naïve expectations that things actually worked out.

As part of our curriculum, we attended the courts. This was great education for me but not for some of the pupils, who knew the court procedures inside out. I remember being appalled by one member of the judiciary who asked a woman to explain why her son had got into such trouble. When she replied, 'I have ten children, Your Honour,' he said, 'We won't hold that against you.' Perhaps I imagined it, but it seemed like he was sniggering. It was clear the dice were loaded against most of my pupils, who didn't respect the law and didn't expect justice. I came to the same conclusion as Mr Bumble in *Oliver Twist* when he said that 'The law is [sometimes] an ass.'

The board worked hard to ensure their pupils were exposed to a broad range of experiences. They invited inspirational speakers from all over the world as part of an international campaign to eliminate poverty and promote peace. It was through this that Jesse Jackson, Seán McBride and Bishop Desmond Tutu were invited to Dublin.

That night in Seán McDermott Street church, when Jesse Jackson had finished, Seán McBride had spoken about Irish history and world history. Even the toughest left the church that evening proud of their community and themselves. Yet nothing of our wonderful event was reported by the mainstream media. In fact, they seemed more interested in publishing stories about violence and drugs in the North Inner City.

The community in that area was in need of good news. It was hard to be proud when drugs were destroying the very fabric of family life. They were being sold openly outside school gates. Young fathers and mothers were dying from drug use and so grannies were rearing their grandchildren. Stories of drug abuse and violence in the area were widely reported. Screaming headlines, portraying violence and crime, were daily beamed into people's homes, making them feel ashamed and isolated.

It was true that many young people from the North Inner City were dying of drug overdoses. It was also true that the same havoc was spreading into more affluent areas, but this was not reported in the media. The valiant efforts of an anti-drug movement, called Pushers Out, were met with hostility from the press. Even though this group was supported by the NCCCAP and Tony Gregory, the media claimed that Pushers Out, which was made up of local parents, had been infiltrated by Sinn Féin.

We found out later that our uplifting event in Seán McDermott Street had not been reported because of much more exciting news. The Fianna Fáil party had attempted another heave to remove their leader, Taoiseach Charles J. Haughey, who was clinging to power like a leech. He was in no doubt that he was Somebody, the only person fit to rule the country. He was a street fighter. Having survived yet another abortive leadership challenge and desperately needing power, he went alone to Tony Gregory's constituency office in Summerhill looking for his vote, which would allow Haughey to form a government. To this end, he brokered a deal with my bosses from the NCCCAP, Gregory, Mick Rafferty and Fergus McCabe. The deal promised £80 million to the North Inner City, which was to be spent on education and inner-city renewal. We thought we had it made. When the deal was done, Haughey shook hands with Gregory, remarking, as the mafia say, 'It's a pleasure to do business with you.' Gregory became a national figure with a dream start to his career.

Haughey soon lost power and the inner city lost £80 million. Still, the people of the North Inner City needed the creative innovative thinking and actions that were provided by the NCCCAP. Our courses were experiential and experimental learning, for all of us. I invited Jennifer to give a workshop on listening skills to the sports group. Mostly tough and streetwise, these were young men who loved combative interaction on all levels. I still thought listening and counselling were the answer to everything. I introduced Jennifer to the group and, sitting myself down at the back of the room, I left her to it.

She opened by telling them a bit about herself, in her clear, posh accent. They were mesmerised and no doubt decided to take the mickey out of her. She asked the group if somebody would like to start by saying their name and something they would like to share with the group. They thought this was hilarious. They started elbowing and egging each other on. I was relieved it wasn't me, but, as I said earlier, Jennifer was no shrinking violet.

Eventually the leader of the pack decided to speak. He was a small, wiry guy with ginger hair and piercing blue eyes.

'My name is Leo,' he said.

'And what would you like to tell us about yourself?' Jennifer asked.

'Just come out of prison,' he boasted, sticking out his chest.

'And what were you in for?' Jennifer asked politely.

'GBH.'

I could hear the sniggers.

'I'm sorry,' Jennifer said tentatively, 'but what is GBH?'

'Grievous bodily harm,' Leo replied proudly. 'One-a them pushers, strung out on gear, got me sister up the pole. Seventeen she was. The brains of the family. Studying for her Leavin'. Died of an overdose. Me ma is minding the kid. Keepin' us awake all night.'

Clenching his fists, he said, 'I shoulda killed the fuckin' cunt while I was at it.'

Jennifer never said a word. Silence reigned.

Leo looked at the group and said, 'What are yis all lookin' at?'

They erupted in relieved laughter.

I wondered how Jennifer might finish. This was no time to ask, 'And what are you looking forward to?'

'Are you all right?' she asked Leo.

'Course I am. I'll kill that fuckin' cunt if I ever get him.'

Some of the group opened up about the prison regime, trying to outdo each other. I think they were hoping to shock Jennifer. They laughed in disbelief when Jennifer said, 'That sounds like Gormanstown College, my son's boarding school.'

Again, I thought of Dad. Only seven years old and locked up in an orphanage. I thought of all the boys incarcerated in Dangan, Letterfrack and Artane. Now these young addicts were being locked up in prisons, because the state didn't know what to do with them, while the drug barons roamed free, unchecked by the law.

Sometimes it was hard to remember that peace, love, joy and forgiveness were possible. My old habits were catching up with me as I tried to save the world again. I was beginning to feel the fatigue of despair that Jesse Jackson had talked about. My stepping out into the world was causing upheaval. I was in need of hope and buoyancy. I was a mouse turning into a tiger. Paddy didn't quite see it that way. Of course, he was right. There had always been a tiger lurking beneath the surface, waiting to emerge.

Our family needed a break. Given that they were now all teenagers, we decided that the kids were well up for a walking holiday in Kerry. We were lucky that we had glorious weather, as we hadn't planned for anything but walking. We got a train to Killarney and walked the four miles to the hostel in Aghadoe. The kids were complaining that it was a forced march. We were struggling, trying to carry all the stuff we had packed. Big plates, heavy knives and forks. A chess set! Nothing as sensible as a torch or a first-aid kit. They stopped complaining about their heavy load when the woman who ran the hostel kindly offered to look after our unnecessary gear until we came back there at the end of our holiday.

At that time there was not so much traffic on the roads. We wandered along the highways and byways. I walked in front. We sang the Scouts song:

> *He jumped without a parachute from twenty*
>   *thousand feet*
> *And he ain't gonna jump no more.*
> *He landed on the pavement like a lump of*
>   *strawberry jam*
> *And he ain't gonna jump no more.*
> *They put him in a matchbox and they sent*
>   *him home to Mam*
> *And he ain't gonna jump no more.*

We could hear Paddy walking behind, shouting, 'Move in. Move in. Car up. Car up.' We weren't going to end up in a matchbox on his watch.

I thanked God we were travelling light as we walked through the Gap of Dunloe into the Black Valley. We had no idea how long it would take. We used the toilets at

Kate Kearney's Cottage near the entrance to the Gap. The jarvies were shouting, 'Do you want a lift?' We didn't have the money to take one of their jaunting cars. Besides, we wanted to walk. Even though the kids were moaning, they were up for the adventure.

We were in fine fettle, refreshed after a good night's sleep in the Aghadoe hostel. The weather was cool, just right for walking. The kids sang another Scouts song:

> *Ging gang goolie goolie goolie goolie watcha*
> *Ging gang goo, ging gang goo.*

After a while we sat on the rocks admiring the view, or at least Paddy and I were admiring the view. We were walking in the narrow gap between two mountain ranges – the MacGillycuddy's Reeks and the Purple Mountains. They seemed to touch the sky, silent and majestic. Sitting in that gap between the mountains, I knew I was a tiny speck, yet part of this landscape. Part of creation, connected to everything and everybody. This must be what's called eternity, I thought. My dad's voice echoed in my head: 'If God is anywhere, he must be everywhere.' I felt grateful for being alive.

The kids brought me back to earth. They were fighting and moaning, 'How far is it to Black Valley?' Thank God we had no idea. We stopped many times on the way, encountering no other travellers. The kids stopped giving out and trudged on doggedly, round and round the never-ending bends. Passing beautiful lakes, crossing bridges, tiny specks on the rugged path between the tall mountains.

Darkness was falling when we spied the lights from the Black Valley hostel in the distance. Oh, what joy! The kids surged ahead of us. They were telling the warden they were starving as Paddy and I stumbled into the reception area.

'Jesus,' I said to Paddy. 'They're making a show of us. Anybody would think they were neglected.'

The kids were already eating Mars bars and drinking bottles of Coke, which the sympathetic warden had given them. We signed in and were shown to our dormitory. Bunk beds had never looked so inviting. We had booked in for two nights. Ahead of us we had a whole glorious day to rest. We cooked a meal with the food we had bought at the hostel store: potatoes, baked beans, eggs. Nothing had ever tasted so delicious.

Everybody in the hostel had to help with the cooking, the washing-up and cleaning the kitchen. I remember Tomás standing proudly between two tall Germans at the sinks. Padraig and Mairead helped to make the bunk beds with a Dublin family we had met at the Aghadoe hostel. The children played games. Our kids were boasting with tall tales of their struggles in the Gap of Dunloe. The other family had travelled by car, which wasn't the same. They were staunch republicans, so we sang rebel songs. They sang 'The Men behind the Wire'. We sang 'A Nation Once Again'. I remembered that when I was young we used to sing 'Starvation Once Again'.

Paddy, with tears in his eyes, sang his mother's song:

> *Oh how sweet 'tis to roam by the Suir's lovely*
> *   stream,*
> *And hear the birds coo 'neath the morning*
> *   sunbeams,*
> *Where the thrush and the robin their sweet*
> *   notes enjoin*
> *On the banks of the Suir that flows down by*
> *   Mooncoin.*

I sang one of my dad's favourite songs about tragic love, 'She Moves through the Fair'. Dad used to say that all our wars were merry and all our songs were sad.

Next morning, we had a delicious breakfast of home-made bread, newly laid eggs and porridge before all the kids went horse-riding.

Tomás and Padraig were raring to go. Mairead was nervous, which was not surprising given that she had never seen a horse close up, let alone ridden one. They were togged out in riding gear. Mairead enjoyed it so much we gave her a present of riding lessons for her next birthday. How lucky we were to have such glorious weather. We explored the Black Valley with the other family at our leisure. The kids were sorry to see them depart in their car the next day, but they were consoled when the local postman offered us a lift part of the way to our next hostel, at Carrauntoohill.

This leg of the journey was easier. Having survived the

Gap, we had gained confidence. We sang all the way to the hostel and arrived there in good nick, probably because we had brought enough water and the right food. The other family, who were seasoned travellers, had given us much-needed advice. When we arrived at Carrauntoohill, we settled easily into the routine of hostelling. We explored the foothills and played football with the kids. We got our gear ready for the next morning and went to bed early.

The next day we attempted to climb Carrauntoohill, the highest mountain in Ireland. It seemed like Mount Everest to us. We were unprepared, as usual. Although we didn't quite make it to the top, we were elated. That night, as we sat eating our dinner, which everybody helped to make, we told ourselves that next year we would do better.

Our next stop was Killorglin. From there we planned to catch a bus to Ballybunion to meet our extended family. Paddy's sister had hired a two-bedroomed cottage, which was to accommodate fourteen of us plus an irritable Corgi called Pidge: he bit anyone who fell foul of him. We got a lift for half the journey to Killorglin. We still had a good hike but, again, sang all the way. We were looking forward to the luxury of travelling on a bus. We sat outside a café in Killorglin, basking in the sunshine, tired but happy. The kids ordered orange juice, buns and crisps. Paddy and I drank tea.

'What time is the next bus?' we asked the lady who served us.

She looked at us in amazement. 'The next bus is not until Tuesday,' she replied apologetically. 'Where are you going?'

'Ballybunion,' the kids shouted. They were dying to meet their cousins. They had had enough of mountains, lakes and valleys. They were fed up listening to us telling them how wonderful it was to be roaming the countryside in the fresh air. Kids these days don't appreciate anything, I thought.

'Oh, that's very far,' the nice lady said. 'It would take you hours to walk.'

The kids started to grumble. They were not going to walk another step.

'Ungrateful wretches,' my mother used to say. Mam was fond of reading and had a lovely turn of phrase.

A lively discussion ensued. The kids told Paddy and me, in no uncertain terms, that they were never going to come on holidays with us again. They used very bad language. Words I wasn't even aware they knew. In counselling terms this meant they were feeling safe enough to express themselves. Paddy was not in possession of this information, however, so he responded in kind. Even in my newly enlightened state, I hoped this wouldn't happen too often.

Tomás suggested that we hitch-hike. Paddy was not happy. He had never done such a thing in his life. It was beneath him. I was embarrassed. The kids had gained a strong sense of themselves after surviving their struggles in the Gap of Dunloe and their 'forced marches'. They were now in no doubt they were Somebodies and demanded their rights. We capitulated. One of many capitulations.

We decided we would have a better chance of getting a

lift if we split up. Paddy, Mairead and Padraig went ahead. Tomás and I stood at the crossroads for half an hour, half-heartedly waving our arms at passing traffic. In the distance I could see the others: they weren't waving their arms.

'Mam, we'll never get a lift like this,' Tomás said. 'What you have to do is this.' Demonstrating, he put out his leg. Then he stuck out his thumb, leaned forward and gave a big cheesy smile. 'You have to look at the driver and smile. I'll hide in the ditch and come out when a car stops,' he said.

No such thing as health and safety. I could have been kidnapped, but as Gran used to say, 'When needs must, the devil drives.'

Tomás retired to the ditch. I was in my shorts. I stuck out my leg, my thumb and anything else that could be stuck out and smiled, smiled, smiled. A big car with an elderly male driver screeched to a halt.

'Where are you heading?' he asked.

'Ballybunion,' Tomás shouted, as he jumped out of the ditch with our two haversacks. The driver was not amused, but I was already sitting beside him in the front seat. Tomás hopped in. The air was a bit frosty.

'Thanks so much,' I said. 'We didn't know there was no bus until Tuesday. We're exhausted after walking from Carrauntoohill hostel. My husband and the other two kids are ahead of us.'

'You're from Dublin so,' he said, accelerating as he passed Paddy and the kids.

He had thawed by the time he left us off at Ballybunion. He was a bachelor farmer called Mick. Three hours later, Paddy, Padraig and Mairead arrived in a taxi. They had walked for hours before taking that drastic step. The taxi cost twenty-five pounds, a large part of our holiday money, and we still had a week to go. We had a great reunion with the families. Pidge didn't bite anybody. We escaped with a few minor skirmishes. Love and joy are possible, I thought.

At the end of our holiday, we stayed again at the hostel in Aghadoe. The chess set was still there! We spent a few days exploring Killarney before packing our gear for the trip home. Renewed, we returned to Dublin.

Back to work on Monday. Another round of courses. I was delighted that Peter Sheridan, a well-known local playwright, agreed to run a course for the young men in the sports group. He asked them would they like to talk about the hunger strike in Northern Ireland which had taken place in 1981 and was still very fresh in everybody's minds. It had been a standoff between IRA prisoners and the UK government. During the strike one of the prisoners, Bobby Sands, was elected as a member of the British parliament, and this attracted the attention of international media. The strike was called off after ten prisoners, including Sands, had starved themselves to death. Peter Sheridan understood how the hunger strikers had become martyrs in the eyes of the young men in front of him. He provided background material and the group was enthusiastic, trying to outdo one another in writing and performing the sketches.

Neil Jordan, the well-known writer and producer, came and showed us his film *Angel* and asked us to give him feedback. Garrett Sheehan, a well-known barrister, facilitated a debate on the upcoming referendum to amend the abortion law. Some people said abortion was about the right to choose. Others said it was about the right to life. We were all learning. This form of education was designed to draw out, rather than impose. It provided opportunities for students to explore and develop their own potential. It was messy. Often we fell by the wayside. We picked ourselves up, dusted ourselves down and got on with it. Education, like God, is to be found everywhere.

My career was taking off. All kinds of strange and wonderful things began to happen. I think this is called synchronicity. I was running freelance courses on assertiveness in Liberty Hall. Some of the participants had set up an Association for Improvement in Maternity Services (AIMS). They asked me to speak on assertiveness in childbirth. This was to take place at the Rotunda Maternity Hospital in front of consultants, doctors and nurses. I couldn't believe it. I was both excited and terrified.

Apparently, it went well. Gabrielle, one of my counselling tutors, said my talk was excellent. She also remarked that my T-shirt, with the upside-down teddy bears, was interesting. I never had any dress sense.

Representatives from the Cork branch of AIMS invited me to speak at their conference in University College Cork. I was beginning to enjoy public speaking. Gabrielle suggested that I might buy a new dress to celebrate. That dress cost a hundred pounds! For days I hovered between the guilt of spending so much money on one dress and the sheer delight of looking at myself in the mirror. It reminded me of my first communion when my sister May had said I looked like a queen.

One Monday morning I received a phone call from a researcher working for *Evening Extra*, asking me to do an interview that day on assertiveness in childbirth. I agreed on condition that the interviewer came to Liberty Hall, where I was working.

'Sorry,' she said. 'I'm afraid you'll have to come out to the studio.'

I'd thought *Evening Extra* was a newspaper.

'Oh. Do you mean the television?' I asked incredulously.

'Will you still do it?' the researcher asked. She had a slot to fill. My name was in the bag. AIMS in Cork had asked them to interview me to get some publicity for its Cork conference. They had forgotten to inform me. I agreed, partly because I didn't want to say no and upset the researcher. This was known in assertiveness training as the compassion trap. I had just fallen into it. A lot of my time was spent climbing out of it. However, in this case I was also curious.

My dear friend Jennifer ran my course that evening. I had my hair done, rang all my friends and had a small nervous breakdown. RTÉ sent a taxi to collect me. I was trembling when I arrived, asking myself was I mad. The researcher put me at ease. I braced myself. Onwards and upwards.

'There's just one other thing I'm worried about,' I said. 'I don't think I can manage the cameras.'

'How do you mean?' she asked.

'You know, when they say, "Take five," and clap the boards and you have to look at the camera. I would find that a distraction.' (I had seen this on the films when I was a child.)

'Don't worry about that. The camera will follow you,' she reassured me.

I was greatly relieved.

'That's not what would worry me,' she mused aloud.

'What would worry you?' I asked.

'All the people watching me.'

I hadn't thought of that!

'That won't worry me. Sure I won't be able to see them,' I replied nonchalantly. How innocent can a person be?

I have no idea what I said on the programme. Whatever it was, the producer was impressed. He said I was a natural performer and he'd like to have me on his show again. I had probably got the taste for performing when I was entertaining the customers in Gran's shop in North King Street.

The Cork conference was a success. Gabrielle said I looked professional in my new dress. Unfortunately, *Evening Extra* was taken off the air the following week. (I don't think it was my fault!) My researcher was shifted to a programme called *Live at Three*. Out of the blue she rang and asked me would I be interested in doing an interview on personal development for her producer, Noel Smith. That meant I would have an opportunity to develop my writing skills. I wrote mini sketches of what I wanted to say and devised questions for the interviewer, so I could cover my subject in the time allocated. The interview went well, and I became a contributor to *Live at 3* over a period of five years.

Now I was in great demand and enjoying my work. Writing, broadcasting, performing and teaching were my natural inclination. Another opportunity came my way when an RTÉ radio producer joined an assertiveness training course I was running in Liberty Hall. Anna asked if I would be interested in working with her on producing programmes on assertiveness for RTÉ. Of course I jumped at the chance. We presented a proposal to the head of programming to produce a series entitled *Speak for Yourself*. My task would be to write the scripts and present the programmes. I did an interview with the head of programming and got the job, even though I'd asked for a fee of four hundred pounds per episode, which was well above the going rate for an unknown and untried person. Anna was relieved. She was afraid I might not get the job because of my accent. At least I had dressed appropriately.

Anna was one of the most supportive, honest people I have ever met. She was a fluent Irish speaker, passionate about the Irish language and passionate about social issues. Our programme went out at an ungodly hour, when very few people were listening to the radio, except perhaps our families. We didn't care. We collaborated in writing the scripts, dealing with issues like the compassion trap and learning to say no. I was learning for myself again and again. Learning that I, too, had a choice to say no, and also to say yes with all my heart. As well as the radio programme, we produced a free booklet, also called *Speak for Yourself*, which was in great demand.

We often had differences of opinion because we were from different generations and backgrounds. Anna was ahead of her time. Not many people had the courage to tackle issues such as assertiveness on the radio in the early 1980s. Some of Anna's colleagues remarked, when they heard my accent, 'You're very brave to have her as your presenter.' Anna received regular complaints about my accent and my diction from the presenter of *Playback*, a programme that played highlights each week. We were dealing with unconscious bias. People from my background were mostly perceived as needing help rather than being radio presenters.

Then I received an invitation from the Women's International Conference to facilitate a workshop on class, accent and language at Trinity College Dublin. A line from the song 'Send in the Clowns' came to mind. Here I was, finding my timing so late in my career. Although Trinity College was in the heart of Dublin, nobody from my family had ever even stood inside the gate. I took my kids for a walk in the hallowed grounds of Trinity to show them where I would be working, perhaps in the hope that it might inspire them to study, enter Trinity and become Somebodies.

The children did not come to the workshop. That would have been far too embarrassing for them. By this time, I was becoming well-known, and that was embarrassing enough.

How best to take the unique opportunity of a small workshop in the grand setting of Trinity – on class, accent and language – and turn it to our advantage? There was not enough time in the two and a half hours allotted to explore the dark shadows that filled us with shame and made us want to deny our roots. I remembered my counselling workshops, where I had learned to take pride in my accent, my class and myself. We decided to celebrate being in Trinity College in a good old working-class way: by having a hooley on the lawn. We danced and sang.

> In Dublin's fair city where the girls are so
>   pretty,
> I first set my eyes on sweet Molly Malone,
> As she wheeled her wheelbarrow
> Through streets broad and narrow
> Crying 'Cockles and mussels, alive, alive oh.'

We danced in a circle, singing 'Biddy Mulligan, the Pride of the Coombe'. I wonder if Oliver Goldsmith, the famous Irish poet, and Edmund Burke, an Irish political writer and a member of the Conservative Party, could hear us from their pedestals outside in front of the college. What might they have thought of our antics? I don't think Oliver would have minded. I remembered him with fondness from my schooldays, a small child reciting his poem 'The Deserted Village'. How Edmund might have viewed our antics I do not know. But, as they say, time puts all things into perspective. I was reminded again of how temporary earthly power is. We all end up the same way. Once more I asked myself, what does it mean to be Somebody? Our antics were not recorded. There were no security cameras at that time. Otherwise, we might have been thrown out and gone viral!

Having made our mark in Trinity, we retired to the nearest pub in Pearse Street and continued our celebrations with more songs. 'Those Were the Days.' Ah ... is this what's called liberation? I wondered. I thought of all the people I knew who never danced on the lawn at Trinity College, who never worked on radio or television programmes or got opportunities to make their mark. I thought of all the people who quietly love and care and share. Unsung, unheard. Surely their sweetness is not wasted even on the desert air.

I thought of the truth in the last line of Milton's poem, 'On His Blindness':

They also serve who only stand and wait.

19

A Peep into the Mirror Within

I could see the three sapphire stones on my engagement ring glinting in the sunlit café as I stabbed the yellow egg yolk with a chip and splattered it over the plate. Dapper in his pinstriped suit, Alex, my fiancé, was gazing at me fondly through his gold-rimmed glasses, admiring my cute table manners and casual hippie clothes. Alex, who came from Inverness, had said I reminded him of a Highland teuchter. In Dublin terms that meant a culchie, which at its kindest could be described as an innocent abroad. Or a right eejit. From a distance, both were accurate descriptions. I could hear Cliff Richard's voice in the background belting out 'Living Doll' …

Images were rising to the surface from long ago. Joyful, carefree, innocent.

'Peggy, where have you gone?' Jennifer called me gently back. She was among the dear companions accompanying me on this perilous inner voyage. We were exploring sexuality at a workshop based on a book called *The Mirror Within*. The course was designed and facilitated by the author, Anne Dickson. Once again, I was taking a deep dive into the underworld, digging in the quarry with my teaspoon, taking a peep into the mirror within. We were learning about images of women in our culture and how they affected us. That scene in the café had remained in my mind all these years. I was back in Glasgow, engaged to be married. A living doll?

'Where were you?' Jennifer asked again.

'Back in Glasgow,' I said. By now, Jennifer knew all my secrets. 'I've cried so many rivers, they should have dried up by now. Are we mad to come on this course?' I asked, as she handed me another tissue.

'We must be gluttons for punishment.' She laughed and gave me a hug.

We were the same age but as different as chalk and cheese. She was tall and glamorous, with auburn hair. I was small, dark and round.

'Where were you when you were twenty?' I asked.

'Travelling the world,' Jennifer said.

I knew Jennifer had been one of the first Aer Lingus hostesses. A picture postcard girl. The Aer Lingus hostesses were like ambassadors for our new modern Ireland. Glamorous, intelligent, with Irish smiles and Irish humour, ready to serve your every need.

'Being an air hostess seemed exotic and exciting,' Jennifer said, 'but it was also hard work. I was in a confined space, serving food and drink. Standing for hours. Looking happy when I was often miserable. I, too, was in love and engaged to be married. John was Catholic. We thought our love would surmount all obstacles, but it couldn't surmount Ne Temere. I would have had to agree that our children would be brought up as Catholic. I couldn't bring myself to do that, not because I was a fierce Prod but because it felt like a kind of blackmail. Besides, our families were opposed to the marriage. It was just too much to handle. John broke off our engagement. There I was, the hostess with the mostest, while struggling to hide a broken heart.'

'Time,' Anne called. 'Let's have a quick round before we go to lunch. This afternoon we'll continue to explore images in our culture.'

A year had passed since this group of fifteen had participated in an assertiveness course, which was based on Anne's other book, *A Woman in Her Own Right*. We had already made a tough journey together. I looked around the group, wondering how their families had survived. Mine were still reeling from the shock of me springing out of the compassion trap. This essentially meant that I had learned to say, 'No.' When I told Paddy I was going to do a course on sexuality, he just threw his eyes to heaven. He was a man of few words. At least there were no men on this course for him to worry about, I thought.

The family had gained some benefit from my assertiveness course. I had discovered once again that I was arrogant. Or, as the Buddha might say, 'There was arrogance in me.' Anne, our facilitator, had delivered this feedback to me while I was having a conversation with her at dinner. I was flattered that she had chosen to sit beside me. I thought she enjoyed my company. Perhaps she did. I wasn't sure what she'd said because of my gammy ear. All I heard was the word 'arrogant'. I nearly choked on my salmon. I had no idea what to say. I think I said I was sorry! We sat in silence for a long time. All my newly acquired assertiveness skills melted like winter snow. Had I been in full possession of myself, I might have said, in my best assertive tone, 'I wasn't aware of that, Anne. Could you give me an example?' Instead, I felt exposed to the world. I thought again of Sheila Fish when her scarf had been torn from her bald head. Was my reaction way over the top? I felt mortally wounded. It occurred to me that I spent a lot of my time feeling mortally wounded.

Jennifer, who viewed me through rose-tinted glasses, assured me, 'There isn't an arrogant bone in your body, Peggy.' She really thought that arrogance was the preserve of the rich. Paddy and my family might have had a different opinion. I thought of how I had sprung myself out of the compassion trap. Of my efforts to save the world single-handed. Of my attempts to reform my family.

I was once again on the familiar path of bashing myself. During my lifetime I had devised many elaborate ways of torturing myself. Yes, of course there's arrogance in me, I thought. I'm not a saint. Yet!

For God's sake, give yourself a break. Sure, you're not that important, I said to myself.

'Jennifer, are we mad?' I asked again, jamming a piece of garlic bread into my mouth. We were having lunch in the pub across the road, which served delicious food. I was grateful to be earning the money to pay for it. 'God only knows what we might uncover this time.'

'At least I know I'm arrogant,' Jennifer replied.

'That is true,' I said.

'Seriously. You have no respect for my feelings, you little brute.' She laughed.

After lunch we continued to explore some of the cultural images of women that influenced us. The Virgin. The Romantic Heroine. The Whore. The Prostitute. Superlay. Madonna. Eve. The Marauding Dyke. She described Superlay, a term she had coined herself, as a whore with a modern face: a woman, free from the risk of pregnancy, always available and exciting. This modern stereotype promised an altogether more sexually active image but was still born of male fantasy and did not represent a woman who was sexual in her own right. I had been wondering what these had to do with me. It started to become clearer as Anne outlined some more information about how these stereotypes affect our behaviour.

We broke into groups of three to explore the different images. My companions were Nuala and Colette. We each took turns to listen, to talk and to observe. I was bursting to talk first. I told them about a picture that was running around in my head of Madonna, strutting across the stage with complete abandon and confidence, singing 'Like a Virgin', which was her latest song. Young girls all over the world, including my own daughters, were singing this song with the same abandon. I feared for them. It was 1984. Contraception was only available in Ireland with a doctor's prescription, and children born outside marriage were still branded illegitimate. Unmarried pregnant women were still being incarcerated in mother-and-baby homes. I did not want to pass on my fears to my dear daughters. Yet my own mother's terror still lingered in my heart.

Nuala spoke next. She was a younger lesbian woman who had dared to come out. She had spent her life hiding, afraid to tell her mother, going over and over in her head how she would break it to her. To her amazement, her mother was not in the least bit surprised. She had known from the time Nuala was a toddler. Nuala said her mother had spent her life worrying about how her daughter was going to survive in such a hostile environment. For now, it was a relief that it was out in the open. 'The times they are a-changing,' Nuala declared with a quiet confidence that gladdened my heart.

Colette said, 'Amen to that. I don't know where to start. I think I must have played all those roles. At first I was terrified of losing my virginity because the consequences would be dire. Apart from becoming pregnant, if anybody found out, you'd be labelled an easy lay. Or you could be called a prick-teaser. I remember courting a boyfriend in his car. I felt something moving down below and I had a look. He had his you-know-what sticking out. I said, "No." Well, to be honest, I wasn't that fond of him anyway. He said he was sorry. Another girlfriend had given in to him, and he had wanted sex ever since. That was the end of him. Eventually I did give in. I was in what is now called a long-term relationship. I thought I was getting married. When my boyfriend broke it off, I was no longer all shiny and new. I felt like a whore, sullied, second-hand. Who would have me now? When I finally did get married, I was so delighted that I turned into a madonna. I just lived for my husband and children. Now here I am. My children have left home, and my husband plays golf. The only role I haven't played is Superlay. I don't have the energy for that now!'

'What a predicament.' Nuala laughed. 'We'd better finish up by sharing something we've learned. Otherwise, we'll all end up in misery. Let's take a few minutes to be still and reflect.'

'I'll go first,' Colette offered. 'My children have left home and John doesn't need me. My parents are dead. Nobody needs me. At first, I was bereft. What was there left to live for? What was I going to do with myself? By chance I received a phone call from an old school friend who was home from America.

'"Are you still writing poetry?" she asked.

'"Nancy," I said, "I gave that up years ago. I never had time."

'"Such a shame," she said. "I was jealous of you. I thought you were so good." She brought me a present of a book of Mary Oliver's poems. It seems very selfish, but now that I've started to write poetry again, I don't have time to mind everybody. I think my family are relieved. John even bought me a book of Seamus Heaney poems for Christmas.'

'How do I sum up what I've truly learned?' Colette said, running her fingers through her long, shiny, streaked hair. 'What I've learned is to live my own life.'

For me the question of virginity had haunted my young life as soon as I became aware of it. I so wanted to be a good girl. I felt I was always walking on a high wire between good and bad. Just listening to the conversations and breaking the wall of silence allowed me to feel as if I was being let out of jail. The other reassuring thing was that none of the other women were telling their husbands about the contents of the course. It's not just me, I thought with relief. Ireland was such a secret society. This was pioneering work. We were slowly lifting the veil of secrecy that had covered every aspect of Irish life. I wanted to do this work for myself and the next generation. I wanted to do it for all generations to come. We finished off the afternoon with a round of sharing what we enjoyed about being a woman. We sang a verse of 'I'm a Woman', made famous by Peggy Lee, joyously spelling out W-O-M-A-N again and again.

Jennifer and I were silent as she negotiated the rush-hour traffic. We were preoccupied with the afternoon's revelations. I wished I had the courage to share them with Paddy and my family.

I was drained when I got home early to an empty house. I climbed the stairs and plopped onto the bed. I howled for the whole poor, ignorant world. For the so-called Garden of Eden Eve had defiled. I lit a scented candle and sat in silence. I was floundering. All my counselling was unearthing so much muck. This journey within was an epic voyage. Despite outward appearances, I was barely keeping my head above water. Oftentimes I was filled with rage, shame and guilt. I was so afraid it would spill out onto my children and Paddy. Why, oh, why had nobody protected me? I would have killed to keep my own children safe.

Then I thought of my parents' generation. They had lived through two world wars, a civil war, the foundation of a new state and rampant poverty and disease. It had all been shrouded in a veil of silence, covered up with lace curtains and respectability.

The scent of the candle filled the air when Paddy opened the front door.

'Your mother is praying again,' he shouted to the kids,

who were coming in the door behind him. 'There's hope for us all yet.'

Everyone was in fine fettle. Marino had won their match. Padraig had scored the winning goal. We celebrated with my pasta bake and chocolate eclairs.

Having explored the cultural myths and images of women, our homework now was to explore our own bodies. The purpose of this was to build our self-esteem and help us develop a positive approach to ourselves, to begin to take pride in our individual beauty, instead of being at the mercy of the prevailing images of the time.

My homework was to stand in front of a full-length mirror and look at my naked body. Just the thought of it gave me goose pimples. For a start, we didn't possess a full-length mirror, and I had never taken the time to look at myself naked. It seemed sinful and vain. I also had to look at my vagina, as Anne Dickson had called what I usually referred to as 'down below'. I do not know what Paddy McManus, or any other member of my family, would have made of me standing naked in front of a mirror examining my vagina. In any event, I did not inform them. Besides, there was no privacy in our house. It was always full of 'Mount Templers', as Paddy called them, because we lived so near the school. Jennifer said I could come to her house when her husband wasn't at home to perform this clandestine operation.

Jennifer's attic was freezing, even with the three-bar electric heater turned on. She had scented candles lighting the room. Beethoven's *Moonlight Sonata* was playing softly in the background. I tore off my clothes, wanting to get it over with as quickly as possible. I felt ashamed and guilty. I was afraid that somebody might see me or find out that I had been looking at myself. I stood shivering, staring at my naked body reflected in the mirror.

I got the shock of my life. Everything seemed to have dropped down, just as my neighbour Mrs Weir-Hart had predicted many years before when I'd told her I was breastfeeding Bride. Since then, I'd had three more children. My once round breasts had turned pendulous while I wasn't looking. They were now perpendicular to the floor. I discovered flesh I never knew I had. My round belly was overhanging my vagina which I still had to inspect. The soft glow of the scented candles seemed menacing, highlighting all my defects. The music was grating on my nerves. I was tempted to run out of the room.

Instead, I wrapped myself in Jennifer's dressing-gown and sat on the bed. I took a few sips of water. I wished I had brought some brandy. I glanced down at my feet. My toes and ankles were all right. I had good legs and thighs. My bum wasn't too bad either. My hands felt nice and soft. I admired my long fingers. I liked my neck and shoulders. I took a few deep breaths and looked again. Strange, I didn't feel so bad the second time. Certainly, I didn't look like a living doll. Anyway, I consoled myself, who wants to look like Barbie in their forties?

My genital inspection would have to wait for another

day. As my mother used to say, 'Enough is enough.' Still surveying myself in the mirror, I got dressed slowly. My body had borne five children: why was I so ashamed of it? Why did I feel so guilty just looking at it? I hoped I wasn't passing on this shame and guilt to my children. I switched off the electric fire and blew out the candles. I turned off the *Moonlight Sonata* and slowly descended the attic stairs. Jennifer was in the hall.

'How did you get on?' she asked.

'All right,' I said. 'I have to rush home. Nobody knows where I am.'

'The nights are growing shorter,' Jennifer remarked, as she drove me to the bus stop.

'Yes. Paddy will be wondering where I am. Thanks for the lift, Jennifer.'

Thank God the bus was on time. In the darkness, the lights of Dublin Bay were reflected in the full tide as the bus drove along Dollymount. Thoughts were swirling through my mind, like the heaving waters. Here I was at forty-five, once again swimming in deep waters, creating trouble, stirring the pot. How could I tell Paddy that I had spent half an hour looking at my naked body in a full-length mirror? My furtiveness would make anyone suspicious.

'Where were you?' Paddy looked up from the game of chess he was playing with Tomás.

'Sorry,' I said. 'I got delayed. I was doing some homework with Jennifer. Where are the other kids?'

'Padraig is at the Scouts. Bride and Mairead are out with their friends.'

'Did you all have your dinner?' I had left a coddle for them. I always made sure I left food for the children and tried to be at home when they came in from school. I didn't want them to be latch-key kids. I worried that I was neglecting them and Paddy. 'I'm off to bed. I still have studying to do for the course.'

I took my *Mirror Within* book to bed with me. I was relieved to read that a lot of women had the same reaction as I'd had. Standing naked and really looking at themselves was overwhelming for many women. Well, at least I'm normal, whatever that is, I thought, looking forward to our next session on Saturday.

We're all in the same boat, I reflected, as I listened to the feedback from the body exercise.

'My breasts seemed to be sitting on my knees,' Mary said. 'I wouldn't mind but I once had beautiful breasts. Thirty-four C. Everybody used to admire them in my V-neck sweater.'

'I don't know what you're worried about,' Molly said. 'Your breasts look good to me. But just look at the size of my belly – I wish I could lie on one of them meat slicers and get a few chunks cut off. I can't get anything to fit me. Why are clothes made for Barbie dolls?'

'Youse think you're bad,' Veronica said. 'Have a look at

my arse. I've spent my life standing with my back to the wall.'

'At least all your bits are covered,' Imelda said. 'What about my nose?'

Beneath the screams of hysterical laughter, I felt sadness. With all the pummelling and bashing, the plucking and dyeing, the dieting, competing, comparing, trying to whip our poor bodies into an ever-elusive shape, we were at the mercy of the fashion world's whims. Even virginity, which was once considered sacred and 'an essential commodity', now seemed to be going out of style.

'Jesus, I hope we don't freeze to death,' I remarked to Jennifer, as we prepared for the massage session that afternoon.

The room wasn't very warm. It was an office we had rented from the Council for the Status of Women. I didn't like having to take off my clothes. I had been in such a hurry that morning, I had no idea what underwear I'd put on. I was still reeling from the shock of seeing myself naked. Also, I had seldom seen another woman naked. I thought of my mother washing at the sink, exposing bits of herself, how shocked she was when she caught me looking at her. How ashamed I was when she gave out to me. Now here we were breaking all the rules of modesty, chastity and respectability. My mother would turn over in her grave. Jennifer didn't mind. She was more liberated than me and was always having massages.

What if Paddy McManus ever finds out about this? I worried he would never speak to me again. I was beginning to learn that silence was the worst form of punishment you can inflict on anybody. Far from being excited and delighted at the prospect of a soothing massage, I was on the verge of a panic attack. The tension was building. Everyone was nervous. Even Jennifer.

Preparing the room brought us back to earth. We began by lighting scented candles and closing the venetian blinds. Otherwise, the respectable citizens of Merrion Square might have thought a sexual orgy was going on. The room was filled with nervous giggles as we covered the floor with our quilts and pillows. Jennifer had brought some for me. I hadn't wanted to explain to Paddy why I needed to bring quilts and pillows to a workshop.

Thank God my partner was Nuala, who was much more experienced than I was. She could see that I was shaking.

'Would you like me to massage you first?' she asked. We peered at each other in the soft glow of the scented candles.

'Yes, please,' I said awkwardly, starting to remove my top. I surprised myself: I was wearing matching black lace pants and bra underneath.

'That looks nice,' Nuala said, opening a bottle of sandalwood oil and rubbing it on her hands.

I lay on the quilt, my body supported by two pillows, my head resting on my hands, listening to the sound of waterfalls. At first it was hard to let go. I kept thinking of my mother, my father, Paddy and even my kids. Gradually

I gave myself over to the music, the scent of the candles and Nuala's kind, warm, loving hands.

We changed places and I massaged Nuala. I became engrossed in what I was doing. All thoughts left my mind and there was just the peaceful rhythm of my hands. When we had finished, I felt relaxed and drowsy.

Paddy was in great form when I got home. He had been out playing golf that afternoon. He had bought a bottle of wine and was making spaghetti bolognese. We were having a family dinner.

'That's a lovely smell,' he said, giving me a kiss. 'How did the course go?'

'Not too bad,' I said. 'Just a bit tiring.'

We went to bed early and I practised a tiny bit of my massage on Paddy before falling asleep.

A pain in my neck woke me. My whole body was shaking. I felt cold and clammy. I could hear Paddy snoring softly. I didn't want to disturb him so I slid out of the bed and crept down the stairs. My stomach was churning, my body shaking. I felt I was choking. I wanted to spit something out. Flashes of images I didn't want to see. Eyes. A tweed coat. Shiny shoes. Hands. A white bedspread. The Carlton Cinema.

I felt I was a bad person even thinking such things. I vomited in the back toilet and flushed the chain. It was like the time I watched my dummy swirling down the pot when I was little.

'Peggy, are you all right?' Paddy called from the landing.

'Yes. I'll be up in a minute.'

Why could I not tell him? Perhaps I was afraid he wouldn't believe me. I could hardly bring myself to believe it. Would he think it was my fault? I thought it was my fault. *Through my fault, through my fault, through my most grievous fault.*

'You're shivering with the cold,' he said, putting his arm around me as I crept back into bed.

'Peggy, you look pale,' Jennifer said, as I got into her car the next morning.

'I was awake half the night. It's horrible the way images keep coming back, just when you think they're gone.'

'Do you want to take some time?' Jennifer asked. 'It's only half seven.'

'No, Jennifer, I feel like I've vomited everything down the toilet. At least it's coming out. I feel very angry towards my dad. Why did he not protect me? How could the possibility not have entered his mind when he asked Mr Adams to stay with us that time?'

'It seems to me that the whole country has been covered in a blanket of silence for years,' Jennifer said. 'Nobody saw or heard anything. The important thing now, Peggy, is to stop blaming yourself.'

Was I ever going to get to the bottom of it? Something was shifting in me towards my beloved dad. I couldn't speak to him any more. He'd always been my hero. I had idolised the ground he walked on. All those wasted years blaming myself, thinking I was a bad person. Since Mam died, Dad had been going downhill. He was an old man now, battling with cancer, and I could find no sympathy for him. How can love just melt away like that? Lines from a Shakespeare sonnet that Dad recited to me had stuck in my mind as a small child, even though I did not understand them:

Love is not love
Which alters when it alteration finds …
O, no! it is an ever-fixed mark,
That looks on tempests and is never shaken.

Oh, how shaken was my love. I had spent my whole life trying to learn about love and how to love. Nothing else mattered to me. Now I knew about trauma and about intergenerational trauma. I worried I had passed my trauma on to my children, just as my parents had passed on theirs to me.

'Jennifer!' I cried. 'Was it all in vain? I want to get out of this hole. How can I find it in my heart to forgive? There is so little time left.'

Jennifer put her arms around me and looked into my eyes. 'Forgiveness,' she said, 'like love, comes from another source. I call it divine grace. All you have to do is be willing.'

I knew the first person I had to forgive was myself. Despite all my trials and tribulations, as my mother used to call them, I also knew I was getting better. If only my mam had had a friend like Jennifer, how different her life might have been. What courage she had shown in the face of adversity. How she had loved to sing and dance.

'Jennifer, you're an angel. I don't know if I would have survived without you.'

'Haven't you done the same for me? We'd better pull ourselves together,' she said, nipping into a parking spot in Merrion Square.

It was our last day. We spent it reviewing what we had covered, what we had found difficult and how we might put into practice what we had learned. I was relieved and sad to be finishing this part of the course, even though I knew I would continue to practise what I had learned for my whole life.

Two major decisions emerged for me. I had decided to go on a retreat. I needed time to reflect and lick my wounds. For some strange reason, I thought of a kitten washing itself in the sun. I also decided to change my name from Peggy to Peig. It was my mam's pet name for me. I envisaged her rubbing my feet when she brought me home from hospital. 'Peig, Peig.' I could hear love in her voice when I was a good girl. The name Peig gave my life a whole new meaning.

What a celebration we had that night. Peggy wasn't to be banished that easily. I dressed up as Madonna in the most outrageous clothes I could find. Jennifer dressed as Maud Gonne. We sang, danced and got drunk celebrating friendship and love. A real Irish orgy.

Jennifer left the car parked in Merrion Square. We threw caution to the winds and got a taxi. I walked as soberly and quietly as I could up the garden path and fell into the flowerbed as I fumbled in my handbag for my key. I made a lot of noise trying to extricate myself from the rosebush. It was Mrs Weir-Hart, my next-door neighbour, who pulled me out. She was a very light sleeper, always lying awake waiting for her husband to come home. My loving family slept through the entire episode. Mrs Weir-Hart rang the doorbell, far too loudly, I thought, waking the whole neighbourhood. Paddy thanked her for her kindness.

He looked me up and down in my Madonna gear and stiletto heels and burst out laughing. The cheek of him. I hung on to the banisters and managed to get to the top of the stairs. I flopped onto the bed in my clothes and lay in a dead stupor until twelve o'clock the next day.

Surprisingly, I didn't feel guilty. Usually, I felt ashamed when I got drunk. I was terrified of turning into my mother. My two brothers, Billy and Martin, had been struggling with alcohol and gambling for years. There but for the grace of God go I.

I had the day off. I dressed myself up to the nines and went shopping. I bought food and champagne, flowers and candles. I made a batch of chocolate eclairs.

'And how is the head, Madonna?' Paddy asked, gazing at the table spread with our best lace cloth, our best glasses, cutlery, flowers and candles. 'What are we celebrating?'

'I've decided to change my name.'

'Not to "Madonna", I hope,' Bride moaned.

'Just tell us and put us out of our misery,' Padraig said. As far as Padraig was concerned, my being on telly was one of the greatest embarrassments of his life. He was living with the anxiety of what I might do next.

'Peig,' I said. 'It was my mam's pet name for me.'

'Like Peig Sayers. I hated her.' Mairead groaned.

'It could have been worse,' Padraig said, breathing a sigh of relief.

'I think that's a great name,' Paddy announced. He loved Irish names.

'What's for dinner?' Tomás asked. 'I'm starving.'

'Pizza, chips, salad and chocolate eclairs.'

'Yum, yum. Pig's bum. Cabbage and potatoes.'

'First of all, let's drink a toast to Peig,' Paddy said. He popped the cork and filled the glasses.

'To Peig!' they shouted.

'Let's hope she won't turn into a Peig Sayers.' Mairead giggled.

'Yeah, she's bad enough as she is. I think I like this champagne. You should change your name once a week!' Padraig said.

We played a game of cards and then we went to bed.

20

Flying

Old memories still bubbled below the surface, but they never had the same impact. Possibly because I was too busy. It was 1984 and I was now working for the Catholic Church at Crosscare, which had originally been set up in 1941 to address the poverty that was affecting wartime Dublin. During the 1970s and 1980s, Crosscare became more innovative, expanding the range of services provided in its centres. My role was to design and run personal development courses in the new parishes that were springing up on the outskirts of Dublin. I met the most wonderful inspirational people, both lay and religious. It helped to restore my faith in the spiritual.

I was also invited to work for the Shanty Educational Project. It had been set up by Ann Louise Gilligan and Katherine Zappone, two feminist theologians who met and fell in love while studying in America. They married in Canada and returned to Ireland, creating the project from their own home in Brittas in south County Dublin. Their aim was to serve the women of the area, enabling them to develop their skills and talents and pass them on to their own communities and families. After all, they were the experts in their own lives. As far as I was concerned, the most important skill for them, and me, was leadership training. How fortunate I was to be involved in such a wonderful enterprise, which had been created out of pure love.

It was Jennifer's doing that I was invited to work on the project. She was involved in recruiting influential people to fund and assist in running it. They raised money to buy buses and collected women from the housing estates in Tallaght, Jobstown and the surrounding areas and brought them to Brittas. The women that Jennifer recruited also made tea and cakes and served our students at break time. What wonderful discussions we had. Friendships were forged across boundaries of class and religion which lasted a lifetime. Liberation theology was beginning to creep into Ireland, opening our hearts and minds.

Getting from Marino to Brittas on three buses was exhausting. It was beginning to take its toll. I decided to invest in a car, which initially Paddy did not approve of.

Gradually, though, he came around to the idea. Travelling along the narrow road from Jobstown to Brittas, I spied the sign for Crooksling where Mam had been incarcerated. So far from her homeplace. So far from her three young children. Oh, my poor mam. My heart broke for her.

How different my life was to hers. How privileged I was. I think it was the courage she passed on to me and the courage and support of so many of my friends and family that had kept me going. Now I had wheels, there was no stopping me. I think this was what Paddy might have been afraid of. I now had a mechanised vehicle to propel me onwards and help me save the world.

I was in great demand on television, the flavour of the month. A kind of working-class novelty. I enjoyed the work but I was beginning to feel burned out. Mrs Weir-Hart, my lofty neighbour, and I had managed to build up a friendship over the years. When her husband died, she asked me to call her Mai. She agreed to work as my housekeeper for two days a week, which gave me some breathing space. Even so, there was always a bit of guilt lurking in the background. My dad was dying, and I was conflicted between family and work. I needed a break. Paddy said I looked washed out. I had intended to go on a retreat, but I couldn't find the time.

Jennifer and Gabrielle had introduced me to a meditation group, which helped me to keep my feet on the ground. In the beginning I was a bit sceptical, but I joined because I didn't want to offend my friends. Also, I was impressed by how they conducted their lives.

Gabrielle became my spiritual teacher. All the people involved in the group gave of their time freely. No money was involved.

The meditation practice was called 'sahaj marg', which means 'the natural path'. It is based on an ancient yogic practice. Mostly it required us to sit in silence and open our hearts to the creator, allowing a space for us to merge with the divine. The group was led by a holy man, a guru, who lived in India. He was our conduit, our connection to the divine. He had trained Jennifer and Gabrielle and they had attended his retreats. They assured me it was a wonderful experience just to be in his presence. They told me that the master, as they referred to him, was conducting a retreat in France. This might be the only time I would ever get to be with him in person. I decided to go.

'That's a great idea,' Paddy said. 'You look worn out. You need a rest. I might go on a golfing holiday. The kids are old enough to look after themselves now.'

'To tell you the truth, Paddy, I'm really worried about Dad. I don't know how long he's going to last, but I must get away. I hope he'll be here when I return.'

'Sure, you can always get back if anything happens. Where is the retreat?'

'In the French alps,' I muttered.

'The French alps? Why could you not meditate somewhere in Ireland?'

'Because the guru is coming from India to conduct the meditation in France.'

'Wait a minute,' he said. 'Let me get this straight. Your father is not well and you're going to pray for him with an Indian guru in the French alps. Are you off your trolley? That sounds like one of them cults. Like the Moonies or the Screamers. They all smoke hash. Sure, they're all completely off their trolleys. That's the crowd The Beatles hung around with. Jesus, what next?'

'I know it's a bit mad. I find it hard to explain, but now is the right time. I've never done anything like this in my whole life. Please, Paddy, I don't know what it is, but I feel compelled to go.' I started to sob. 'It's to do with my dad.'

Paddy put his arms around me. 'Okay, Peig. You have to do what you have to do. When are you thinking of going?'

'Next Monday.'

'So, you had all this planned behind my back?'

'I'm sorry, Paddy, but I was afraid to tell you.'

'Jesus, what next? Well, you'd better start getting ready.'

'Jennifer has booked my tickets and Gabrielle is bringing me to the airport.'

'That pair are beginning to be a bad influence on you. They're starting to lose their halos. I wonder what their husbands think about them wandering all over the world following strange Indian gurus.'

Gabrielle told me about the ashram as we drove to Dublin airport. It was in the mountains outside Nice, near the village of Tourrettes-sur-Loup. I was flying into Nice.

'Sometimes people from the ashram come and pick you up but don't depend on it,' she said. She had been there many times. 'It's in a wonderful old farmhouse high up in the mountains.' She described a long bus journey around hairy mountain bends. I was both thrilled and terrified. This would be my first excursion to the continent on my own.

The flight was delayed. When I arrived in Nice airport, the daily mountain bus had departed. It was hard to find anyone who could speak English. After some time, I managed to establish that a train was leaving from Nice in two hours' time that went to a nearby village. I caught the bus into the city and proceeded to look for the railway station. Even with the help of a French phrase book, which I had bought in the airport, I couldn't make myself understood.

With ten minutes to spare I saw a group of people with trolleys. They were walking towards me, wearing sahaj marg meditation badges. They were an international group and some spoke English. I explained my predicament. They too were heading for the ashram and invited me to join them. They took me to their hearts and shared their food and drink with me. They kept trying to make conversation. All I could say was, '*Merci. Merci.*' My gammy ear and the strange accents were contributing to my confusion. I pretended to fall asleep.

One train, one bus and a taxi journey later, we eventually arrived at the ashram around midnight. Everything was in darkness. We were greeted by a woman carrying a torch. She whispered that her name was Victoria. She was Mexican. She was going to take us to our rooms. She put her fingers to her lips. 'Quiet,' she emphasised. 'Everybody ees asleep and they will keeell us if we wake them up.'

I knew they were not literally going to kill me, but those people sounded a bit over the top, especially for a group who were there to practise love and peace. Victoria pointed the way to a bed in a darkened room. I could make out other shapes around. Gently I placed my trolley on the floor. I got into my nightdress and slid into bed, hoping I wouldn't need to use the toilet. I lay still as a mouse and mercifully drifted off.

The sun streaming through the window must have woken me. I could see the dawn rising, lighting the mountaintops. The world was awakening. In a corner of my room, a tall man with a long grey ponytail was sitting in the lotus position, facing the rising sun, and meditating. I must be having a vision, I thought, but when I opened my eyes again, he was still there.

If Paddy McManus ever finds out about this, I'll never be allowed out of the country again. How am I going to get dressed?

'*Bonjour*,' Victoria called from across the room. 'This is my son Carlos,' she said, introducing a young boy who looked about ten years old.

'*Bonjour*.' He waved.

'We're getting ready to go to the meditation hall,' Victoria said as she picked up their neatly folded clothes from their beds and headed for the bathroom, which was at the other end of the dormitory.

The man in the robe also took his clothes from his bed, turned towards me and silently saluted, *namaste*, which I knew was a blessing. He was the handsomest man I had ever laid eyes on. Imagine being blessed by him. I lay in bed, stunned. There was absolutely no possibility of me ever becoming a saint! I lay on, gazing at the sun moving across the mountains. The room was sparse: bare wooden floors, long windows with no curtains, four beds and lockers. Now that I was in this beautiful silent place, I felt at a loss. I didn't know what to do with myself. I felt my aloneness, my foolishness. Why had I come here and what was I searching for? I began to drift back into sleep.

The sound of voices awakened me. Quickly I jumped out of bed and grabbed my clothes. I washed and dressed in the small shower room. Pulling myself together, I set forth in the direction of the noise. Hundreds of people were seated at long wooden tables bathed in glorious sunshine. They were eating bread, cheese, fruit, pasta and vegetables. Families, grandparents, teenagers, middle-aged and older people. The babble echoed across the mountains and down through the valley.

People had come from all over the world. Some were casually dressed, others in their native costume. The laughter, the splash of colour, the smell of the food. Such a celebration of life. People pushed up to make room for me at the end of a bench. I poured myself a bowl of hot chocolate. Having stepped into an enchanted world, I was feeling a bit out of my depth. I sat there taking it all in, hardly touching my food. People attempted to engage me in conversation, but I couldn't understand their accents or hear through the noise. Still, I was drinking it in, immersed in the overall joyfulness and goodwill.

After lunch I helped clean the kitchen. There was much banter between the women as they cleared the tables, washing and drying the dishes and cutlery. Everything was done by hand. I remained enclosed in my own bubble, not quite ready to join them. They respected my silence.

We were free to spend the next three hours, between noon and three, as we pleased. I went back to the empty dorm and lay on the bed. I had never been so truly alone with myself before. My head ached. Strangely, I felt the weight of the world on my shoulders. I washed my face and went out to where the children were playing. Watching them for a while, I thought of my own children when they were young. Memories of my brothers and sisters drifted by. I could hear their joys and sorrows ringing in my ears. I pictured little Peggy always trying to be good. Once, we had all been children. In a way, we're always children in this ancient universe, vulnerable and fragile.

I wandered across to the meditation hall where people were sitting in silence, preparing for evening meditation with the master. Taking my place among them I sat, hoping my heart would open. The hall filled and the master arrived. We sat for another hour. I would love to say I was filled with bliss and love and forgiveness. Instead, my mind was full of thoughts and worries that I was supposed to observe and let go. Towards the end of the meditation, I caught a glimpse of stillness.

When the session was over, I made my way back to the kitchen and helped to serve the evening meal. Once more, I stayed in my bubble. After dinner I joined the women again and we cleared up. In the evening we had conversations with the master, who answered questions about the practice of meditation in everyday life. I was not yet ready for this. I even found it difficult to say the word 'master'. Yet I thought it was wonderful that hundreds of people could sit in silence, willingly allowing their hearts to be opened. I wandered around, listening and watching, feeling my aloneness. I went to bed and fell into a deep sleep.

Next morning, I woke with a headache and was sick. Victoria brought a doctor to see me. He looked at my tongue, felt my pulse and gave me some small white pills to be taken in water over the course of the day. He told me to go outside and sit in the sunshine. Later I learned he was a homeopathic doctor. This encounter led me in later years to train and become a homeopath.

As I sat in the sunshine, people approached, asking how they could help. A lot of them spoke English. They were surprised to learn that I was Peig from Dublin. They had mixed me up with a woman they were expecting from England, who was very sick and did not want to be disturbed. They had been wondering why I was working in the kitchen. Over the course of the day, I was sick again. Sleep came over me.

When I awoke, feeling refreshed and hungry, Victoria and the tall guy were standing at the end of the bed. I sat up and they gave me some water.

'This is Rolf,' Victoria said.

'My name is Peig,' I said, stretching out my hand.

'Peig,' Victoria said, 'when you arrived in the darkness, I mistook you for someone else and I did not like to disturb you. How are you feeling? You look much better now. Would you like to come to meditation with us?'

'I'd love to.'

After the meditation, I felt a bit lighter and joined Victoria, Carlos and Rolf at the dinner table. Rolf was German. He was fascinated by the name 'Peig'. He had never heard it before. I was fascinated listening to all the different languages – European, American, Asian, African, Australian. This meal, this gathering, is a holy communion, I thought. I felt blessed. Wouldn't it be good if all our world conferences could begin with an opening of hearts? After dinner Rolf asked if I would like to go for a walk in the mountains. The sun was setting and the air was filled with the scent of the wild mountain flowers which were covered with water droplets after a sudden shower. We could hear the sound of goats' bells.

'Peig, do you think it's possible to fly?' Rolf asked, as we stood gazing into the gorge below.

I was puzzled. I'd never thought of that before.

'Do you think it's possible?' I asked.

'I think all things are possible,' he said.

239

What a wonderful dream. I wished it were true. I hoped it was true. I thought of my dad, sitting on the toilet in Cabra, in the only quiet place he could find, transporting himself to any part of the world while chaos reigned downstairs. Sometimes he sat there just for the sheer joy of it. Flights of imagination, I thought. My mam used to say I lived in my imagination.

'Yes,' I said. 'I think it is possible to go to other worlds in mind and spirit. I can imagine myself flying across these mountains. But maybe my body needs a little more training. My feet are too firmly planted on the ground.' I laughed, breaking the spell.

'Would you like to come to sit with the master?' Rolf asked.

'I'll try it. Sure it won't kill me,' I said.

Sounds of laughter came from the packed room as Charjii, the pet name for the master, told jokes. What a pleasant surprise. He seemed smaller and more human than I had thought him to be. There were discussions on the different stages of consciousness, which were way above my head. We moved on to the practice of meditation in everyday life.

The practice of sitting in silence each morning, with an open, loving heart, helps us to be present in whatever we're doing during the day, whether it's cleaning the toilet, working in the kitchen or walking in the mountains. Each evening we sit in silence, letting go of the clutter we've accumulated. This helps our minds to become peaceful and calm. With practice, we can learn to tap into this pool of peace, even in times of great stress. Over the course of my life, I have found this to be true.

'Master, may I ask a question?' I asked, raising my hand.

'Of course,' he said, smiling.

'I am a bit puzzled,' I said hesitantly.

'Continue.'

'I thought meditation would help us to lead a more balanced life.'

'This is true.' He nodded.

'I'm sorry to ask but why are there no men working in the kitchen?' I felt the change in the room. I've put my foot in it again, I thought.

The master looked perplexed. I don't think it had ever occurred to him. After a few puzzled minutes, he spoke of the ideal of service. The kitchen was the women's domain and he more or less said, 'Each to his own. Now let us move on.'

There was silence. No one else asked any questions.

'Thank you, master,' I said.

We concluded the session with a meditation.

'Peig, you've certainly made an impression.' Rolf laughed as we made our way back to the dormitory.

'God, I hope I haven't caused any trouble. I didn't mean to. This seems to be my lifetime's mantra.'

Next morning after meditation, a deputation met the master. The kitchen was closed. There is no breakfast, they told him. Discussions followed. After all, this was an international gathering and the women considered themselves equal to men. A rota was established and everybody became involved in the running of the ashram. To me, this was meditation in action.

I kept a low profile. I knew I wasn't there to make waves or save the world. What a relief to have its weight lifted from my shoulders, temporarily at least. That had been a bit of an addiction, and I continue to learn this lesson. I spent most of my free time playing with the children or wandering along the mountain paths. I knew I needed to be alone.

In the evenings I spent many hours listening to the master. I learned a lot about the discipline of meditation, about observing thoughts, treating them like uninvited guests, how not to entertain them so I wouldn't be at their mercy. I realised how often I disturbed my own peace, making mountains out of molehills, as my mother used to say. How cruel I was to myself. I longed to take little Peggy and tell her she was always good in her heart. I knew the peace that lies beyond all understanding lay within. I did not have to fly anywhere to find it.

I was ready to return to Dublin. Rolf drove me to Nice. The family were waiting for me at Dublin airport. I had arrived home just in time to be with Dad before he died.

21

My Mother Threw Me off the Train

Memories of old wounds melted in the mists of time. My dad's voice echoes in my head. 'What a glorious day'; 'Come watch the dawn breaking'; 'See the moon rise'; 'Look at the stars'; 'The Big Plough and the Little Plough.' He sang, 'Sleep, love, it is not yet the dawn, angels guard thee.' My dad's motto had always been 'Face up to reality'. He instilled this in us from a very early age.

Now he was facing the reality of his own death.

'I wonder what the next leg of the journey will be like,' he said, as he lay dying on the sofa in our small parlour in Cabra West.

'I know why people rob morphine,' he said, as he popped

the tablet into his mouth. 'I take my tablet, switch on my electric blanket and fly away to all the places I dream of.'

In his lifetime, he had devised many ways of flying away when the storm clouds were gathering in the wake of the turmoil he had created. His method of rearing children was to throw us into the sea. We soon found out whether we could sink or swim. Mostly we swam, and so we learned to chart the great ocean that is called life. This was a trick my dad had learned from the Christian Brothers, in whose tender care he had been reared for eleven years. He also received a first-class education.

In his final years he was blessed. Susan and her husband decided to move in with him. Dad was delighted with the company and enjoyed a second chance of love and laughter with his little grandson, Eoin.

'I don't mind dying,' he said. 'Sure, nobody will miss me.' He knew how to press all the buttons. He was a bit of a rogue.

'I will miss you, Dad,' I said. 'We will all miss you.'

His voice still echoes in my head: 'What a glorious day.'

In his younger days, he had raged and raged against his predicament: an educated man among *amadáns*, which, of course, included us.

'Face up to reality,' he would rant. 'Have some sense. Wake up.' ('Wake up' was another of his favourite expressions.)

We had no idea what he was talking about. Now I think he was talking to himself when he lost his wages on a dead cert and stayed in the pub because he couldn't come home to face reality. Yet he mellowed and went gently into that good night. He found peace, despite the storm clouds that were still gathering and building in our family. In his final hours in the hospice, I sat with him, listening to his breathing, not laboured or gasping but like waves lapping on the shore. I counted each breath and heard the rhythm of death. Silently we forgave each other.

I sang his favourite songs, 'She Moves through the Fair' and 'My Lagan Love'. Then, like a small bird's wings fluttering, he was gone through that portal. The same one he came in, the one through which we continuously weave in and out in this dance of life.

With our dad's death, the fragile bonds that bound the family were shattered. Our wounds surfaced and the family secrets began to tumble out. After the funeral, my sister May pressed a small black-and-white photo into my hand.

'Dad asked me to give you this,' she whispered. It was a photograph of my baby girl Marie, who had been born twenty-three years before in 1961, in a Glasgow maternity hospital. This was the photo and letter I had requested from the adoptive parents, which I thought had never arrived. I had wanted to see my baby for the last time, to find out what kind of people I was handing her over to, before signing the adoption papers. Every day I watched for the post until finally I gave up. My distraught parents must have watched me waiting for the letter. They must have been relieved when I gave up watching and signed the adoption papers. Not a word was spoken.

It should have been the most natural thing in the world for May and me to look at the photo together and maybe put our arms around each other. It should have been perfectly natural for me to ask my sister, 'What did Dad say when he gave you the photograph?' Why could we not bring ourselves to speak?

May had been so kind to me after Marie was born. She had taken me in when I arrived on her doorstep in England, raw and wounded. I was not an easy person to be around. May was only a child herself, recovering from a difficult birth. She had developed an abscess while breastfeeding her three-month-old daughter. On the day of her marriage, she had gone to live in a strange land, just getting to know her new husband. Yet they both treated me with kindness and tolerance. May must have been in pain as she listened to me. She cried with me as I wrote and rewrote a ten-page letter to Marie, trying to explain why I'd decided to have her adopted. Now, twenty-three years later, we could not look each other in the eye as I silently slipped the photograph into my handbag.

My parents had kept that photograph hidden for all those years. Was it under my dad's pillow that time we talked in the parlour just before he died? Mam had gone to her grave with this secret. Did she ever look at the photo? Did they ever wonder about their granddaughter? Perhaps they had decided it was not in my best interest to see the photo. Perhaps they imagined that if I saw my baby, I might want to keep her and might refuse to sign the adoption papers. Were they trying to spare me the pain? Dad, on his magic carpet, could not bring himself to share the photo with me even after all these years, though it must have been on his mind that time when we had sat in the parlour. How little we truly know of one another.

Such shame and disgrace I brought upon the family as an unmarried mother with a baby born out of wedlock. At all costs my younger brothers and sister had to be protected from the disgrace. Otherwise, they might be tainted by the scandal and end up going astray. Our family was a fragile entity, adrift in stormy seas, trying to cope with mental illness, tuberculosis, alcoholism and gambling, struggling to present a respectable, acceptable face to the world. As the oldest child, I was expected to set a good example and be responsible. I wanted to be good even from an early age. I absorbed all the tensions of the family. I wanted to make it better.

Despite her illness, Mam was determined to live to rear us. She used to say, 'I'll do it or die in the attempt.' When she was well, she cooked delicious meals with the cheapest food. Even though she was very sick, she still sang to us. She had a lot of sayings: 'Let us be grateful for small mercies'; 'A little help is worth a lot of pity'; 'Dust thou art and into dust thou shalt return.' Her advice on matters of love was, 'If you don't have respect for yourself, nobody else will.' Life wore her down and she took to drinking to ease her pain. Chaos reigned supreme. I tried to hold things together, but I didn't know how. I became chief bottle-washer, a mini tyrant, a little bossy boots, a righteous, royal pain in the arse.

I thought I was on my own. But I wasn't. Looking back, my sister was always at my side. Like all my siblings, May felt the tensions in the family as much as I did. We clung together for support. We wanted to escape. For most women, the only escape at that time was marriage. We thought we might live happily ever after, despite the evidence of our own eyes.

Of course, I had the additional burden of having to save the world. I've already mentioned that, at seventeen, I joined the Legion of Mary with my best friend, Maureen. Now memories of that experience came flooding back.

The aim of the organisation was to help 'the neglected and the rejected', as Frank Duff, the founder, described them. It was a worthy cause. Dublin was filled with the rejected and neglected. Frank's heart was in the right place. Maureen and I went to work in Harcourt Street Hostel as part of a street rescue team. We learned what life was like for the women who worked on the streets. It was a harsh and cruel occupation. They were just ordinary women, many of them unmarried mothers, rejected in respectable society. Our job was to befriend them, to let them know somebody cared for them, two very young, skinny, virtuous little girls in stiletto heels hobbling beside them on their beat during the long winter nights.

Walking along Burlington Road, Leeson Street and

Hatch Street, Maureen and I linked arms under the shadow of the trees, imagining someone was going to jump out at us. We were terrified and thrilled at the same time. It was like seeing a Dracula movie. We watched the women get into big cars. Mostly they were ill-clad and shabby. After an hour or so, the women would return to their spot. Although we were supposed to be rescuing them, we didn't really know what we were rescuing them from or what they were doing in the cars, except that it was a mortal sin. We were foolish, naïve and a bit of a nuisance. Many times, the women would shout at us in desperation, 'Go home. Get away from here, ye little scuts,' as we tried to invite them to the hostel for a cup of tea. We were hell-bent on rescuing those poor unfortunate women, who mostly just wanted to get rid of us.

From a distance of sixty years, I can only imagine my parents' fear when they read the letter that contained the photo of my child. I was on the verge of signing the adoption papers. They were afraid I might change my mind. They need not have worried. I had decided to have Marie adopted. I was a fallen woman, damaged goods. Who would have me? That was what my parents thought. That was what I believed. The worst possible thing for my daughter was that she would be branded illegitimate, a bastard. I could not bear such a life for her. We might end up on the streets, like those women in Harcourt Street.

The photo my parents had kept hidden for twenty-three years was now zipped into the pocket of my handbag. I still hadn't found the courage to tell my other children about Marie. Even my closest friend, Maureen – who was with me when I met Marie's father, Alex – knew nothing about her. Only my husband, Paddy, knew about Marie. He had married me despite my shame. Paddy was a righteous, kind, reserved man. It pained him to know I had a child with another man. There was an unspoken agreement that my child would never be mentioned again. She lay, like an open wound, between us.

Now there was another family to be protected. How could I tell my four teenage children that they had another sister, aged twenty-three, born in Glasgow? How could I show the photo to Paddy, which might bring to light the open wound that lay beneath the surface and perhaps ruin our fragile peace?

My fumbling efforts to tell my story to my children, show them the photo of their sister and talk to Paddy were met with silent embarrassment. Who in their teenage years wants to know about their mother's past affair? Paddy did not want it dragged up. My dad had just died, and my immediate family was in turmoil. Nobody wanted to know.

Still, it never occurred to me that I had the right, or indeed a duty, to look for my daughter. Having signed the adoption papers, I had signed away all rights. In my mind, my duty to my child was to accept the instruction of the adoption society, which was to sever all connection with my daughter to allow her to bond with her new parents. Having given her into their care, I had to make a clean break and allow the loving parents to raise Marie as their own. In my heart I believed this was true. It made sense to me. I had lived with this belief for so long now, I didn't have the courage to continue pushing through my family's wall of silent embarrassment.

Years later, when I met Marie, she was in her thirties. She was pregnant with her first child and had been looking for me for seven years. She was about to hire a private detective to find me. Now that she was expecting, she desperately wanted to know who her parents were.

Strangely enough, I only found the courage to look for Marie in 1994, after my first grandchild was born, out of wedlock. Our adored Holly was welcomed into our family with open arms. She melted my numbed heart. Memories of Marie's birth in a Glasgow hospital in 1961 came flooding back: a Saturday afternoon during a thunder and lightning storm. The pain, the stitches, the joy when I held her, the savage, primitive impulse to protect her. Nothing else mattered. I remembered Mam telling me she counted my fingers and toes when I was born. I counted my daughter's fingers and toes. Fiercely I held her, determined to keep her.

In desperation, I wrote to my fiancé's mother, Isobel. She travelled from England to Glasgow to see me. She had no idea about my situation and was devastated. 'This is my first grandchild,' she said, as she held Marie in her arms.

Isobel was not ashamed of her. I think she felt sorry

for me. I didn't want pity. Alex was on board a ship bound for South America. Isobel sent him a telegram telling him that I was thinking of keeping my baby. Alex was not overjoyed. Isobel did her best. She might have taken me to live with her, but I was so confused I didn't know what to do. She wrote to me for a few months, but I never saw her again. Many times I thought of writing to her to tell her what had happened. How awful it must have been for her never to know, but I was afraid it would upset my marriage if she wrote back, afraid Paddy might think I was trying to make contact with Alex.

When I first met Alex in the Locarno Ballroom in Glasgow, that night in 1959, he swept me off my feet. Even though Maureen was wary of our whirlwind romance, she was happy for me. This was what we had both longed for – a chance of a new life, an escape from home. I would escape from Dublin, where people were defined, classified and sometimes dismissed because of their accents and where they lived. Nobody, I thought, could label me by my accent in Glasgow. I might have a chance of getting a decent job, maybe even have a career. Imagine.

At that time, respectable couples did not live together or have sex before they were married. Alex found me a room with a girl called Patricia whose fiancé, Jeffrey, was a college friend of his. Patricia was reserved, contained and fastidious. She was also an only child and not used to sharing her space. We slept together in a double bed. I was messy, untidy and untamed. Not at all house-trained. Within a week, my clothes were strewn over the bed, under the bed and on all the chairs. Alex introduced me to vodka, sex, jazz, art and all his classmates, who thought I was wonderful. Naturally I lost the run of myself.

Patricia was horrified and too respectable to fight. A cloud of polite intolerance descended. She and I made life hell for each other. Patricia clung in silent rage to her side of the brass bed under a heap of my clothes, which were draped above her on the headboard. She finally erupted one night after I had awakened her out of a deep sleep at half past three in the morning, as I drunkenly tried to ease my way into my side of the bed.

She was crying and screamed, 'You have changed into a brazen hussy.'

This was true, but it was just a solo run. The brief mad flight of a firefly. The truth was I was lonely and lost, adrift in stormy seas. A bad, bad girl. How easy it is to fall from grace.

Once again, I joined the Legion of Mary, in Glasgow. I became part of a house visitation team, calling on old people. This helped to assuage my own loneliness and isolation. Alex and I were drifting apart. Reality was beginning to dawn on both of us: it was not working. Yet I was somehow tied to Alex. I had given him my most precious possession, my virginity. Even though it had probably happened in a drunken stupor, it was sacred to me. Now I was sullied. Nobody else would have me. At that time, the sole purpose of my life was to love and be loved. To be respectable. To get married and have a family who might go to college and have a better life than mine. Why I thought going to college should make a person happy is a mystery to me now.

I became pregnant. We were both terrified. For me, marriage now seemed to be the only respectable option. Alex did not want to get married. We agreed the best course of action was to have the baby adopted. Alex went back to sea. Patricia's fiancé, Jeffrey, also went back to sea. Patricia went home. There was no question of me going home. I found another room and continued working as a clerk in a hire-purchase office. I sent threatening letters to customers who bought furniture on the never-never and couldn't keep up with the payments. When it became obvious that I was pregnant, I was politely told to leave my job, and also my room. I seriously considered suicide and bought the tablets.

Somehow I managed to stay afloat. I was learning to swim in the deep ocean. I went to confession in Glasgow Cathedral, to cleanse my soul. The priest was a kind old man who was also involved in the Legion of Mary. My story was a familiar one. He made arrangements for me to go into a mother-and-baby home. I had no idea that such places existed. Such wilful innocence.

The home for unmarried mothers was run by nuns who were kind and humane. It was tucked away out of sight on the outskirts of Glasgow. It accommodated twenty mothers and their babies. There were five dormitories. Each dorm had four beds and four lockers. There was just enough space to hold four women. I shared a dorm with

Norma, aged sixteen, who had become pregnant when she and her boyfriend, also sixteen, experimented after reading *Lady Chatterley's Lover*. It was about a sexual affair between a gardener and a lady. Norma found it hard to believe how easy it was to get pregnant while she still had her knickers on.

Then there was Jessie, who occupied the bed opposite me. She was twenty-two and expecting twins. Too tiny to be carrying such an enormous bump. She was an orphan, raised in a convent by the same order of nuns who ran the mother-and-baby home. When she left the orphanage, she was homeless and lived on the streets. Jessie was as tough as a nut. She pointed to her bump and said, 'I could have had an abortion, you know.'

'What's an abortion?' I asked.

'Well,' she said, 'the doctor said he could have got rid of the twins before they became babies. Anyway, I didn't want to do that.'

Oh, so that's what abortion is, I thought. I might have considered that had I known.

Claire, a countrywoman from Ireland, occupied the other bed across from me. She was thirty. A teacher. Imagine. I never thought this could happen to a respectable person like a teacher. Her baby's father was married with three other children. Claire educated us all in many ways, and me in particular. Chaos had followed me to the home. My clothes began to cover the top of the bed, under the bed, the window ledge and the top of the locker. Claire was the spokesperson for Jessie and Norma. They had all agreed. My things were going into the bin if I didn't tidy up. No sulking was entertained. Order was restored.

Part of my maternity care involved being tested for venereal disease. I didn't know what this was, but I had a sense that it was something shameful. The clinic was in the heart of Glasgow. It seemed like a dark, sinister place. It reminded me of the dark places in Dublin. I could hear the echo of my stiletto heels and see the long, narrow hall in the Harcourt Hostel, with the statue of Our Lady perched in the fanlight above the door. I could smell the stewed tea Maureen and I used to make in the kitchen for the women who had come in out of the cold. How little we knew.

My details were taken. I was given a number, 31, and ushered into a waiting room, where four other women sat silently. Nobody looked up when I came in. Nobody looked up when the nurse called number 31, took me aside and told me I was clear. I travelled home on the bus with all the normal people, knowing I had escaped something awful. When I got back to the room, Claire was sitting on a chair knitting a cardigan. I flopped onto her bed, sobbing.

'What is venereal disease?' I asked.

Claire put down her knitting and sat on the bed beside me. She put her arm around me and said, 'It's a sexually transmitted disease.'

'Why would I be tested for it?' I asked.

'Peggy', she sighed, 'how could you be so innocent, and you from Dublin? Unmarried mothers and prostitutes are usually tested for sexually transmitted diseases.'

I told Claire about Harcourt Street and the women Maureen and I had tried to rescue. She laughed and said, 'Sure aren't we all in the same boat now?'

Claire, Norma, Jessie and all the other women in the home were my saving grace. Tucked away from society's gaze, we created our own commune. Of course there were rows, skirmishes, silences and hierarchies, but we were bonded by our predicament. Endlessly we talked about our babies, their fathers and our families. We went round and round in circles, telling our stories over and over again, while we knitted baby cardigans, hats, mittens, socks, dresses and shawls, and got our layettes ready to give to the adoptive parents. We wanted the best for our babies: a nice home, a good education, a respectable family. Respectability was out of the question unless we had our babies adopted. We swapped our maternity dresses as we grew bigger and waited for our time to come.

Jessie had two beautiful baby girls. Norma had a boy, ten pounds. I had Marie, seven pounds two ounces, and Claire had a boy.

Now we were busy in the nursery, bathing, feeding and changing our babies. Morning, noon and night we talked about how we could keep them. The high point of our day was the rosary, which was recited by Sister Catherine, a lovely doddery old nun. Our laughter echoed round the nursery as we lost track of the Joyful, Sorrowful and Glorious Mysteries, the Our Father, the Glory Be to the Father and the Hail Mary. We sat between the rows of baby cots and recited:

Hail Mary, full of grace,
The Lord is with thee,
Blessed art thou among women
And blessed is the fruit of thy womb, Jesus.
Holy Mary, Mother of God,
Pray for us sinners,
Now and at the hour of our death. Amen.

We were so used to reciting the Hail Mary, we didn't realise what we were saying. Such innocent laughter.

There was much rejoicing when Norma's parents took her and her baby home. There was such grief on the day the adoptive parents came for Jessie's twins. Claire and I bathed, changed and fed the twins and got them ready for collection. We watched from an upstairs window as the nuns handed them over to the adoptive parents. Jessie couldn't bear to be around and had gone to the pictures in Glasgow with a friend. The nuns found a place for her to stay and she left the next day.

Claire was determined to keep her daughter, Grace. She had her fostered for a year, while she went back to Ireland to try to find a way of keeping her. Marie was also fostered while I came home to try and persuade my parents to take me in. But I realised I didn't want to bring her back to the place I had run away from.

After the adoption, I received a final letter from Alex looking for a photo of Marie. On the back of his mother's telegram he had reconsidered the situation and he was now writing to ask me, once again, to marry him. It was too late. I had made my decision. I turned down his proposal of marriage. Perhaps he was relieved. Though his intentions had been honourable, our love had fizzled out.

Now, it was 1994, thirty-three years later, and my 'legitimate' daughter Bride had a baby girl born out of wedlock. We were overjoyed. Scenes from the Glasgow mother-and-baby home nursery came rushing back as I watched Bride feeding Holly. I cried for Jessie, Norma, Claire and all the other mothers, and for myself and Marie. I became very sick and could no longer put on a happy face and pretend that all was well. All the years of silence and shame suddenly seemed so mad, so futile, so sad.

I spoke to Gabrielle, my long-time counsellor.

'Peig,' she said, 'I think it's time for you to look for your daughter.'

Somebody had given me permission. This time I found the courage to speak to Paddy. Breaking the silence was awkward and messy. At first, Paddy didn't want to talk about the past. It was too painful for him. But I could not, would not, live with the silence any longer.

For years, I'd had nightmares of Christ crucified but I never told a living soul. Now our granddaughter was bringing us an opportunity to heal our wounds and make a fresh start. Both of us were willing. We took the risk and said out loud the awful unspoken things we needed to say to each other. Wonder of wonders, we survived. I never realised that Paddy was suffering as much as I was. We agreed it was time to find my daughter. Paddy wrote to the adoption society in Glasgow. They replied by return post and sent us some documents, which included the letter I had written to Marie, explaining why I had decided to have her adopted. Written in bold letters across the envelope were the words 'DO NOT DESTROY'. The adoption society also put us in touch with a mother-and-baby link in Edinburgh. They got in touch with Marie, who had been trying to trace me. How easily I might have let her go. Our dear Holly was a divine messenger.

Very soon a letter arrived from Marie. She was over-joyed that we had found each other. She was married to a Greek man and expecting her first baby. Marie asked me to meet her in London. Outwardly I was delighted and excited but underneath I didn't know how I felt. I hadn't allowed myself to feel for so long. Paddy wrote to Marie, welcoming her into our family and asking her to be kind to me.

When I saw her, I was so shocked. Looking into her eyes was like looking into my own soul. I could see myself in Glasgow all those years earlier. She looked so like me, even the way she stood, balanced on one foot. She was six months' pregnant and still managed to be gorgeous. I was wearing my sackcloth-and-ashes look. I don't think she was impressed on that score. Marie probably takes after Alex, who was a very classy dresser. She was delighted to hear that she had two brothers and two sisters and was looking forward to meeting Paddy.

Marie had one brother, John, who was fourteen when

she was adopted. John left home when she was very young. She was reared as an only child, doted on by her parents and a large extended Catholic family. She didn't know she was adopted until she was fourteen. Her dad tried to tell her about her adoption and give her the letter I had written. She refused to read it and freaked out. She became angry and ungovernable and didn't want to know anything about me. Her dad returned the letter to the adoption society. How easily it could have been destroyed. Thank God some thoughtful person decided it was important enough to keep.

Marie had been reared in a housing estate in Glasgow, very similar to where I had grown up in Dublin. I had been hoping for a nice, leafy, middle-class suburb for her, and a university education. At that time, I associated being middle class and educated with happiness. Marie had managed to make her own way in the world. She was a highly successful lawyer, and she also had the gift of a happy nature. I was in London when she had her daughter, Clea, a few months later.

Of course, there were difficult times. Now that Marie had her own child, she asked how any mother could give away her own baby. She would never give her Clea away under any circumstances. That was a question I had lived with all those years. I struggled to put it into words. The nearest explanation I could find was in a book I was reading at the time, which I had found in Marie's library. It was written by Bruno Bettelheim, a survivor of the Jewish concentration camps. The book examined why so many

Jews had died when, he believed, lots of them might have escaped. One young man was asked how he had managed to survive when so many others had perished.

He answered, 'Because my mother threw me off the train.'

Such a shock of recognition for me. That was exactly the way I'd felt.

22

Go in Peace

Bride and Bert got married. One of my friends decorated the church. It looked like a harvest festival with lush fruit and red, gold and yellow decorations. Holly and Saoirse, Bert's daughter, attended their parents' wedding. Imagine.

Marie, my long-lost daughter, arrived with baby Clea, our latest granddaughter. Her Greek husband, Vassilis, also came with his mother, Kettie. Marie met her siblings, as well as her aunts and cousins. They were all a bit overwhelmed, but they thawed over the course of the wedding celebrations. Paddy was relieved to meet Marie at last, and he fell in love with her. She had been an unspoken shadow throughout our marriage. Her presence gave

Paddy and me an opportunity for acceptance, healing and forgiveness. We were blessed. This was to be Paddy's first and last time to meet Marie.

Paddy was not well. He was feeling low. Having taken early retirement from his job with Eircom, he wanted to stay at home and look after the house, but it didn't suit him. He was lonely and isolated. Missing the structure and the camaraderie of his work, he became reclusive and depressed, not wanting to leave the house. Bride's wedding, as well as finally meeting Marie, brought him respite and joy.

It was coming up to Paddy's sixtieth birthday. He was adamant that he was not going to have a party. As I look back, I remember what a rich social life we had, with many parties, card games and family meals, gatherings with aunts, uncles, cousins and grandparents. I'm so grateful for it now. After some persuasion from me, Paddy reluctantly agreed to a small family celebration. He hated being the centre of attention. By nature, he was a quiet, shy man.

We sang our hearts out. Paddy's family were great singers and performers. That night, Paddy even danced a jig with his sister Polly, which he had not done for years. Later he thanked me and said it was the best party he had ever had. We were all relieved.

Two weeks later Bride, Holly and Bert moved to County Clare. We were delighted for them setting up their new home, although both of us were heartbroken to lose them, especially Paddy. Seeing Holly had become the high point of his week. She had stayed with us overnight on Thursdays. He had fed her, changed her and played with her all day. He loved to spoil her rotten.

After his sixtieth birthday, Paddy, who had already been deeply depressed, sank down even further. Four days later he died of a heart attack on a golf course in Newlands Cross, surrounded by his old school friends. Such a wonderful way to go. Such an awful shock for us. My poor dear family, whom he loved so deeply, were devastated. I was numb, even though I had had a premonition that he was going to die. I had watched him fading away since he had left work. I'd wanted so much for him to enjoy his retirement. He always said he was looking forward to becoming a house husband.

The morning of the day he died, as he stood at the sink washing his golf balls, I said, 'Paddy, you're breathing very heavy.'

In a rare confession, he said, 'I feel under pressure. I don't feel up to playing.'

He had been persuaded by his friends to go on a golf outing when they'd met at the funeral of an old school pal. They'd talked about their adventures and lamented that all their friends were dropping like flies.

'Let's get together and have a day out before we all pop our clogs,' someone had suggested. They were sitting in a nice warm pub, well soused.

'That's a great idea,' they all enthusiastically agreed, and arranged to meet on 4 December.

It was a freezing cold day. Paddy didn't want to let them

down. Not recognising how anxious he was, I encouraged him to go. I was so delighted he was going to meet his friends.

'Paddy, you'll enjoy it when you get there,' I said, helping him to get his gear ready.

He gave me a peck on the cheek and ran out to the waiting car. After he left, I realised we hadn't blessed each other with holy water from the font. This had always been our custom, through fair winds and foul.

December 4 was also Tomás's thirtieth birthday. I was cooking a family dinner, steak with all the trimmings. After work, I drove into town to get my shopping. I parked in a lane off Capel Street where I used to park when I visited Bride, who had lived nearby. It was about three o'clock and I felt a sense of unutterable sadness and desolation. I thought it was because Bride, Holly and Bert were gone. Now I think it was the moment when Paddy died.

Paddy's oldest friend, Joe Doyle, rang me to deliver the news. 'Peggy,' he said, 'Paddy has collapsed on the golf course and I think it's serious.'

I knew this was Joe's way of telling me Paddy was dead. Cool and calm, I put down the phone and switched off the cooker. As I crossed the road to get a taxi, I met Mairead, who was just arriving for Tomás's birthday party.

'Mairead,' I blurted out, 'Dad is dead.'

Now I think, How brutal. But despite my calm exterior, I was in total shock.

She said, 'I don't believe you. Why are you not crying?'

I was dazed. We got a taxi from the Malahide Road to St

James's Hospital. Joe had spread the word. All the children and Paddy's siblings were there. Everyone was in total shock. Paddy was still warm and we said prayers. A priest was administering the last rites. My most vivid memory is of Mairead, Padraig, Tomás and me putting our hands on Paddy's warm body and saying, 'Go in peace.'

When we got home, our milkman called to collect the weekly payment. He was deeply shocked and spread the news of Paddy's death as he went from house to house. Paddy was well known and popular. Our house was quickly filled with neighbours, friends and relatives, who brought food and drink. They took over and minded us.

Bride had no phone. The guards in Clare got one of her friends to go with them to break the news. We were all wrapped in a cloak of kindness.

We got Paddy's body home the following morning. We didn't want him lying in the cold morgue. Father Tom, Paddy's brother, an Augustinian priest, arrived from Florida. Bride and family drove from Clare through a black, icy fog. Paddy was laid out in the front room. With Father Tom, we blessed him and sprinkled holy water. We said prayers, not quite sure of what to say. No words seemed adequate. We sang hymns and held each other for comfort. We were delighted to have him at home. I am sure his spirit remained for those three days when we waked him and celebrated his life.

Jennifer, my dear friend, stayed in our house for the three days, praying and grieving, singing songs and telling stories with us. She had never seen an Irish wake. I watched her, hands entwined in rosary beads, kneeling at the coffin across from our very holy neighbour who was giving out the rosary. Jennifer was so impressed she said she wanted a wake when her time came. We gave Paddy a royal send-off.

Afterwards, all was quiet. We were in the depths of winter. The trees on Griffith Avenue were stripped bare. Everything seemed bleak and desolate. We had walked for all our married life along the avenue, to school, to church, to holy communions, confirmations, weddings and funerals, without us noticing that the trees were constantly reflecting the passing years. Paddy's hair had turned from jet black to silver. Our children had grown into adults. I used to admire the bare branches against the grey sky. Now all I could see was bleakness and desolation.

Paddy and I had sailed together on a journey that had lasted thirty-three years. Sometimes we were in calm, safe waters. Many times we had sailed through stormy seas and almost capsized. Paddy was my best teacher in life, and I think I might have been his.

The house was so empty. All the family except Padraig had left home. That Christmas we all came together again and celebrated. We talked about Paddy, who had loved Christmas. He always insisted on us wearing those awful paper hats. Even Mam and Dad and the old ladies who lived next door had to wear them.

It was a good Christmas. We were all determined to make it work.

New Year's Eve. Silence reigned. This was it. My first time to spend New Year's Eve alone in my whole life. I drank a few vodkas, watched telly and listened to the bells ringing in the New Year. One of my neighbours, trying to console me, had said, 'I know what it feels like. My husband died ten years ago. You'll never get over it.'

In my heart I knew I would get over it, though I was afraid I might take to the drink to ease my pain, as I was inclined to do. The family limped along and we supported each other as best we could, each grieving in our own private way. I was too fragile to keep running groups. However, I did continue to study homeopathy, which I was passionately committed to, and passed my exams.

My meditation practice, prayer and friends carried me through. I meditated on death and dying, thinking of my dad, who had said, 'I wonder what the next leg of the journey will be like.' I knew Paddy was at peace. I could hear his soft, gentle voice humming 'The Rose of Mooncoin'. I could see him running through the fields in his bare feet during his summer holidays in Ballyragget, County Kilkenny, his mother Annie's homeland. Perhaps this is an idle dream, but I trust in the spirit that exists within and beyond this earthly world.

My sixtieth birthday crept up on me. The family organised a surprise party in the big function room at the top of the Conservative Club building in Camden Row. My sisters and brothers, whom I had not seen for years, were there. It gladdened my heart. Bride, Tomás, Padraig, Mairead and I stood on the stage and sang our song,

'Donna Donna', about the calf being led to slaughter and the swallow flying free, and neither knowing why. Please God, I hoped my children had learned to fly.

As for me, I was soaring. I had fallen in love again at sixty. My foolish heart. Frank made me laugh. It was like being a teenager again, carefree and wild. He could be rude, crude and sometimes ruthless. Not the kind of man for your sixty-year-old mother to be roaming the world with. To me he was kind, romantic and he loved me.

I already knew him well. His wife Marie had died around the same time as Paddy. She had had a lot of sickness. We used often to go out as a foursome to plays and concerts. Frank had helped Paddy run his charity quizzes.

I threw caution to the wind, as my dad used to say. I left my community in Marino and went to live with Frank in a beautiful new house he had built on a nature reserve beside an estuary in north County Dublin. I turned down Frank's offer of marriage without explaining why. I didn't even know why myself. Now I think I was afraid of getting married for fear it might spoil the magic. Also, I would be giving away my freedom. With hindsight, this was a mistake, even though we did make legal agreements about what should happen to our assets when we died. Marriage is a sacred commitment on a spiritual level and helps us to face the ups and downs of a relationship.

My new home was idyllic and isolated, but I missed my family, friends and my Marino community.

I thought Frank would like to have children around him, but he didn't want the disturbance. He didn't understand them. He still lived in the world where children should be seen and not heard. That made it awkward, as I was blessed with eleven gloriously boisterous grandchildren whom I loved passionately and longed to spend time with. My dreams of happy family gatherings did not materialise. Frank had a strange sense of humour. Periodically he would announce, 'I love children. Sure I have one every morning for my breakfast.' An old joke from a black-and-white movie, his laughter skidding around the table like broken glass.

I decided to spend as much time as I could with my family without Frank. We had holidays all over the country. I loved doing mad things with my grandchildren. Dancing in the dark, pushing them on swings until they stopped screaming, 'More!' Jumping in puddles, walking on walls, reading stories. Watching them in the water. Watching my children playing with their children. I remember walking my grandsons Joseph and Matthew to school. I was holding their hands, about to cross a busy road.

'Peig.' Joseph looked up at me earnestly. 'I know everything. I was here before.'

Joseph was always saying things like that; I think he was an old soul. He died tragically aged sixteen. Perhaps he was only meant to visit us for a short time. He left us a gift of love. I'm so glad I got to spend that time with all my grandchildren.

Otherwise, Frank and I got on well together. We introduced each other to new interests. Frank was a passionate conservationist and a community activist. I introduced him to counselling, meditation, homeopathy, drama and my family. We both loved music and dancing. And travelling. We roamed all over America, Asia and Europe for ten years, using the Lonely Planet Guide. Frank introduced me to bird-watching. We could wait for hours in the wilds of Australia hoping to catch sight of a rare bird.

'Listen to those birds singing,' he used to say. 'That's God's orchestra.'

We led a carefree, adventurous life, but I missed the everyday occasions with my family and my grandchildren. Still, as Mam used to say, you can't have everything.

The tide was out and the Brent geese were feeding on mudflats at the edge of the estuary behind the house on the morning Frank got his terrifying diagnosis of bowel cancer. It was on my birthday in April 2011. His consultant delivered the news over the phone and made an appointment for Frank to see him the following month. Frank couldn't bring himself to believe it. The word 'cancer' struck terror into his heart. At seventy-seven, he was still a vigorous, youthful, black-haired man. He wasn't ready to die. He went through an agonising month waiting for his appointment, becoming silent and withdrawn.

Frank was relieved to hear that his cancer was very treatable. 'We got it early,' the consultant reassured him. 'Just a small growth. It's a simple operation and you'll be good for another twenty years.'

It sounded glib to me.

'That's rather optimistic,' I said, 'given that Frank is seventy-seven years of age.'

I had put my foot in it, again.

After the very simple operation, Frank lasted two and a half difficult years. His lovely sunny temperament gradually changed during the course of his intense chemotherapy treatment. He became paranoid and aggressive, believing that my kids and I were after his money and land.

We still listened to music, while I massaged his feet at night. We walked every day when he had the strength, but nothing consoled him. Spring, summer, autumn and winter merged. He couldn't even hear the birdsong. God's orchestra had stopped playing for him. He was becoming so angry and terrified of dying that it was hard to reach him. Sometimes I wanted to strangle him. I remember as a child wondering why I had to pray for the grace of a happy death. Now I knew.

Death struck again. That winter Bert, Bride's husband, had a heart attack while they were watching telly in the sitting room. After surgical intervention, he survived five weeks on a life-support machine. I was with Bride when she agreed to have it switched off. We both said to Bert, 'Go in peace.' Bride was now a widow with three young children.

Perhaps Frank's love of nature sustained him as he lay dying in our sitting room. From his window he could see the dawn rise, the sun lighting the trees in the evening, darkness coming on and the leaves falling. He had a bird's eye view of the nature reserve he had created.

We had a camera in a bird box that was connected to the telly. Each evening we would sit and watch a great tit coming in to roost. She flew in earlier and earlier as the days grew shorter. We would hear the tap as she landed on the roof of the box. We watched as she scrunched and wriggled her way inside. This took about half a minute – a delicate operation. Then she would mooch into a comfortable position, tuck her head under her wing and sleep. We could see her every breath. The tiny fluttering, beating heart, which could be snuffed out at any minute. I felt the three of us were connected to the heartbeat of the world. So fragile. I knew how little control we had over anything, including death.

Frank did go gentle into that good night. I sat in a chair away from him watching the rhythm of his breathing change. I longed to put my arms around him to comfort him, but I was afraid I might interrupt his journey. He went to sleep in the arms of morphine. I was glad for him when he died. Peace from the awful battle he had waged against death. Bert, my son-in-law, was also at rest but my dear Bride, Joseph, Holly and Matthew were still in the midst of grief. How could I answer Matthew's question, 'Peig, why do people die?'

I think I said, 'Matthew, everything dies but it comes back again. Like the flowers.'

I retreated inwards, seeking solace in silence and the darkness of winter. But everything changes and the light crept in. The trees began to bud, and the birds were singing their hearts out. Nature was shouting, 'Wake up! Wake up!' How could I ignore such joy?

Finally, the Brent geese were getting ready for their long journey back to the Arctic. I could hear them cackling on the shore. Frank used to say they were having union meetings. They had a few practice runs and then they were off in V formation.

Easter came, with its promise of resurrection. Now I understood what resurrection meant. I could see birth, death and rebirth happening before my eyes in my own garden. I was ready to face the world again. I got involved in setting up an active-age group and started learning to play the ukulele. I enjoyed it. My family joked that I was upsetting the grandchildren and the dogs. The cheek of them.

Covid arrived. Fear seemed to permeate the whole world and we were forced into lockdown. Death tolls from Covid were broadcast daily by the media. Long lines of dead bodies were shown nightly on the telly, terrifying people who were trapped in their homes, isolated from their loved ones. We never heard about the millions who had recovered.

I got Covid during the early weeks of lockdown. At first I thought it was just a cough but gradually I realised it was the wretched virus. I treated myself with my own remedies. I recovered, recuperating by walking out along the sea every day and enjoying the glorious weather.

Having faced death in all its different guises, I wanted to live and help other people deal with this mass psychosis, as the Covid time is sometimes referred to. The world's media and some branches of science tapped into our fear of death and magnified it. I made fun videos for the Fingal Older People's Council. I played my ukulele and danced in the waves outside my house, defying the ban to stay indoors.

It was time to write my memoir. What a truly delightful task. It had been percolating for eighty years. With the help of my friend Helen, I managed to master the computer. Every morning I lit a candle and asked for guidance. I did my qi gong exercises. Afterwards I tackled my writing, tapping away with one finger for two hours. Then I gave my brain a rest while sitting in my porch, watching the seasons change.

In September 2022, as I was watching the leaves fall, I got a pain in my chest. It did not go away. I must be having a heart attack, I thought. I'm just going to sit here in the sunshine, look at the trees and die. Silently I sat and waited for death to come. It did not arrive and the pain in my chest grew worse. I knew I needed help.

Who is the maddest person I know? I asked myself. Debbie. She was a friend I had made at the ukulele group. She'll know what to do. I managed to ring her. I just said, 'Debbie.'

She knew by the sound of my voice. 'I'm on it,' she said. Techno language. Five minutes later she arrived in a buttercup-coloured dress. She had been on her way to a ukulele session. I explained that I was having a heart attack and I just wanted to die in my own home.

'That's okay,' she said. 'I'll sit with you.' Then she

muttered, 'The trouble is, though, you might not die. You could last for a long time, but you may be left staring at the ceiling for years. Let me call the ambulance and they'll know what to do.'

The prospect of being left looking up at the ceiling for years did not appeal to me. Modern medicine has mastered the art of prolonging death, as well as saving lives. The ambulance arrived pronto. The two paramedics introduced themselves. John and Toby, who was Polish, helped me to walk into the ambulance. They did an ECG test.

'I have good news and bad news,' John explained. 'The bad news is that you are having a heart attack. The good news is it's fixable. I've sent a photo of your heart into the Mater Hospital. They're waiting for you. I'm going to give you something for the pain.'

The team were waiting for me when I arrived. Efficient, kind and courteous. They saved my life.

Next morning, I unhooked myself from all the tubes. I needed to go to the toilet. I felt alive and well. I came back to my room and sat on the chair beside the bed, noticing the bright blue walls of the tiny ward. I felt totally at peace with myself and the world. I was glad to be alive, even though I had been quite prepared to die. My time had not yet come, my earthly task not yet done.

Acknowledgements

I would like to thank Helen Reidy, my friend and colleague, who, with gentle persuasion, facilitated the birth of this book. And to Joan, who was with us on this journey.

I would also like to thank Mary Farrell, who encouraged me in the writing and promotion of this book.

Then there is Jonathan Williams, my agent, whose first editing put me on the right track. To Ciara Considine, my publisher, who believed in me, and to all her team at Hachette. Thank you all.

Much gratitude to my family, who still manage to love and support me despite my fragile state while writing this.

Throughout my life, I have been very blessed by the friendship of so many inspirational people who have left me such a wonderful legacy of love. I hope their voices continue to echo throughout this book.